Rhein Dahler

BEFORE

THE

SPOTLIGHT

Tom,
To a great competitor
and a fantastic player.
We have a lot of great
By Drew Rogers
memories to
share!
Bill Moulder

FIRST EDITION, PUBLISHED BY FULL COURT
PRESS, JUNE 2013

Copyright © 2013 by Drew Rogers

ISBN-13: 978-1489517005
ISBN-10: 1489517006

Cover art by Erin Sharpe
Cover design by Jacob Rogers
Interior design by Cate Crayton
Promotion and marketing by Zachary Rogers

Printed in the United States of America

Dedication

In memory of my mother, for all of the scrapbooks, without which I never could have pieced this story together. I went looking for episodes, but found myself back in her lap, the familiar press of her chin against my head, paging through a lifetime of memories so meticulously glued to the withered pages. She taught me the celebration of each event—won or lost—for the simple act of sharing, for how we played the game.

Essence of stillness
Players, a game, nothing more
Before the spotlight
        -Yo Itzin, Haiku Master, 1688

Prologue

The 1960s are remembered as a time of change, the architects thereof ranging from hippies to war protestors to civil rights leaders. Race riots spread through many U.S. cities in 1965 and would continue through the end of the decade creating war zones within the very borders our country had secured against outside invasion. Change in the 1960's was much more aggressive and violent than the popularized peace marches and sit-ins of hippie lore. It was a time when blacks were still knocking on political and social doors in vain, a time when 'separate but equal' represented good intentions gone awry.

Change as it was labeled invaded the sports world as well when boxing heavyweight champ Muhammad Ali refused induction into the army in protest of the Viet Nam war and black athletes protested during the 1968 Olympic Games. In February of 1972 a mostly black University of Minnesota basketball team mugged Ohio State's white center, Luke Witte resulting in the eruption of a race riot that would invade college sports irrevocably.

On March 11th, 1972, barely a month after that college brawl, two teams took to the floor to contest the Missouri State Class L high school boys' basketball championship. Raytown South High was an all-white team from Kansas City. Kirkwood High, from the St. Louis area started three blacks and two whites. Both teams endured race riots following their respective quarterfinal games causing Raytown South to seriously consider withdrawing from the tournament altogether. Nervous Raytown South administrators finally acceded to state official pleas to continue, but their semifinal game against all-black Sumner High from St. Louis was moved into a daytime slot as a hedge against potential violence and to mollify players and fans.

It was a time of racial strife throughout the United States and despite their young age, all of the players who took to the floor that night were affected by issues normally confined to adults and politicians, issues that were thrust upon them by the events of those times. The game served as a vortex, drawing young men on disparate paths together for just one night, to play in front of thousands of fans who watched and thousands more who listened on the radio. The event itself was just a single game but the story swelled with coincidence, opportunity, race and dozens of other behind-the-scenes forces. I started at center for Kirkwood High that night. And this is the story of our team.

Chapter 1

The locker room at old Brewer Fieldhouse is dark and dated. The fixed, wooden benches are worn to a shine, polished by a million butts before us. The rails and floor bolts are painted a putrid, shiny green. The tarnished lockers are crisscrossed by dim shadows from the faded glow of the caged light fixtures. It's just twenty minutes before we're to take the court for pregame warm-ups, but the locker room is crowded with various intruders to our pre-game prep—reporters, other coaches, even other high school players, perhaps in Columbia for recruitment by the University of Missouri. I came down for a recruiting trip myself just a month before, played pickup games with Mizzou players while the coaches looked on, sizing me up. My ankle was still sore back then, fresh out of the cast I wore while my torn ligaments healed. I wasn't moving very well that day, but I shot it just fine. I could always shoot it.

Crowds gather in our locker room tonight because it's the state championship game. We're one of only two teams still playing, so I suppose it's no surprise that people are congregating here. There's nowhere else to be. All the other players are done; so are the coaches. Even the high school beat reporters are out of other stories. Ours is the only story left to write.

I don't think about any of that right now. I just think about the game. I'm not nervous and I'm not nostalgic. I have no sense that this is the last high school game I'll play. In junior high I used to put three sweatshirts on and splash down the street in jeans and sneakers to play two-on-two on a cramped driveway court with Don Bertram, Bill Tice and Seth Whitman. We'd push the snow and ice aside and slip around trying to get some bounce out of the vinyl ball, which was hard and slick from the cold air. All that mattered then was the game, not winning or losing, just the game. That's all it's ever been to me: another chance to play. And that's all tonight is too.

Kevin King appears. I met him at the Ed Macauley hoop camp in southern Illinois the summer after my sophomore year. He was talented but mostly he was a hard worker. I had drifted over to the gym the night I arrived at camp. The program's activities weren't scheduled to start until the next day. It was a Sunday night in an abandoned gym in the middle of nowhere. I decided to shoot around a little because I was bored. But not Kevin. Kevin was in there doing drills when I arrived and he was still doing drills when I left. I was good because I was tall and athletic. He was good because he worked his ass off. Nick Adzick was voted top camper after he led everyone in scoring, but he didn't get jack against Kevin when they played. Kevin's team won em all that week because he ran the show right. Adzick became a good player for Clayton High. Kevin was All Metro for CBC his senior year. I've no idea where he'll go after high school but I'll bet he'll be a big success—real hard worker.

But Kevin never made it to this game. "Man, I'd trade every honor I got this year to be in your shoes," Kevin tells me. He stares at me with eager, ravenous eyes, his leg twitching like he has to pee. All that hard work just to make it to this game. I get that. But I lack any regard for his envy or his frustration. It's just another game.

2

Our coach, Denver Miller, stands just outside the locker room, smoking and jawing with a couple of men I don't recognize. They're not reporters; maybe they're old friends. He seems distant, I suppose because he's out there talking and he's not in here pacing. He's just BSing with a couple of old guys. Then again, I don't really know how he's supposed to act. He's been to this game before and I haven't, not unless the previous two years spent sitting in the stands counts. He lost his previous state championship game. We all know that. He says his 1961 team was the best he ever had and that irritates me a little. We're 31–0 and favored to win tonight. His '61 team lost in the regular season and lost in the quarterfinals. How can he figure they were better? It doesn't matter. We'll win tonight—win the final, win the championship. I think he expects to win tonight, too, but we can all see his anxiety. He's out there kibitzing because he's scared as hell.

I glance around the locker room. It's the thirty-second time we've laced them up this season. Counting back to my sophomore year, that's more than eighty games together for a few of us. We've always been loose, protected by the ignorance of youth, but tonight we're all tossing furtive glances around like a passing drill. Tommy, Robert, Jesse, Billy—they're all absorbed with uniforms and shoelaces, simple tasks suddenly complicated by distraction and circumstance and, yeah, just possibly nerves.

Billy's not scared. I know it because we roomed together last night in the hotel after winning our semifinal game. We talked deep into the night. We've been talking and playing together for two years now—Mr. Outside, the junior point guard, and me, Mr. Inside, the senior center. Our girlfriends snuck up to our room just to hang out for *an hour or two, to revel in the moment. Just four high school kids in a cheap hotel room creating an adventure.*

Billy glances my way and nods, then he looks across at the others. They've still got their heads down, lacing their shoes, silent. Any other night, Robert would be in one of his moods, carrying on or sulking. Tommy would be moving around, loosening up, maybe teasing Sam Weaver with his "Uncle Wheatley" patter. But tonight, not a word. Locker Room Smith mentioned on the bus ride over that Tommy found out we had girls in our room and was mad. But that's the kind of stuff that's never said aloud, real or imagined. So there's no telling if it's nerves or resentment. It's just real quiet.

The locker room door opens and the noise from the sellout crowd erupts, forcing itself in, filling the locker room, and sucking out the former stillness like a giant vagrant in from the cold. Mr. Miller shoos away the remaining stragglers and pushes his shoulder against the squeaky door, closing us off as the noise abates, muffled and distant, but still beckoning. Our coach pauses at the blackboard, grabbing a piece of chalk, his back to us. He stares at the board, gathering himself, and I'm thinking, "We're undefeated. This isn't even the best team we've played this year. Relax..."

The rhythmic stomping of feet on bleachers pervades the dim room like a pulse, more than a noise. Mr. Miller puts his hands on his hips, and watching his back, we see his shoulders rise and heave as he takes a deep breath. Just another game. That's all. Just like slosh ball in the neighbor's driveway...

Mr. Miller turns, his eyes on his feet, the chalk loose in his hand. I really don't care that it's the state final. I never cared, not like that. I used to pretend. I'd make up games in the fading light before

4

dinner, shooting all alone on a neighbor's hoop. Olympic gold medal game against Russia, taking the last shot against Boris Badenov...Mr. Miller draws another breath and then sighs, raising his hand to the blackboard.

"Well, boys…"

Sometimes I'd drain that last shot, send Boris and Natasha and all the other Russians home to their babushkas and their vodka and invite the onrush of adoring hordes. It was just a game, just, in fact, my imagination. The shot was real, but the game was not. And sometimes, I'd miss that shot…but I'd been fouled. So I'd step to the line, needing one to tie and two to win. Sometimes, I'd drain those free throws to the delight of the US contingent, but sometimes I'd miss…but then I'd grab the rebound because there were still two ticks left, and I'd soar over Boris and make the put-back, and so the United States still won, and I still prevailed. There was always another chance.

It's just a game, always has been. That's all tonight is: just another game.

Isn't it? Isn't it just another game, like slosh ball and Drew versus the Russian Olympic team? I don't know, I don't know, I don't know.

The Game

Many a tear has to fall,
But it's all
In the game.
> –"It's All in the Game," Carl Sigman (sung by
> Tommy Edwards)

There's The Game and then there's the game. The Game is an event, an occasion with uniforms, fans, cheerleaders, bands, coaches, referees, reporters, circumstance, history, subplots, programs, agendas, outcomes, consequences—a contrivance.

The game is simplicity. It is you and me and a ball. It's a test that rewards preparation and talent and just plain old who's better at this moment when I put the ball on the floor to get to the hoop and you move your feet to stop me, maybe you reach in for a steal, and maybe I punish you for your lunge, crossing over and getting a step, and then you recover and go for the block, guessing I'll take it straight up, only I'm ducking under to put it up on the other side, and we both drop to the floor and glance up and see that it's in and it's my point and it's winner's out, so you grab it as I line up at the top of the key. It's 1–0 and we both know it, so you don't say it. I say, "Ball," and you get in your defensive stance, taking away my right side before you toss it, or maybe you just hold it there so I have to reach over and take it, and you say, "Check." The game is pure.

The game exists within The Game; it is the pearl within the oyster. The game is players and The Game is everything else. That's not to say that the players are privileged or elite, because any of us are entitled to player status whether the game is basketball or checkers, and whether we're good or we suck. The game is an opportunity.

Nothing affects or alters the game. Once you kick away the gravel, straighten the rim, establish the boundaries, or shovel off the snow, there's the court and you and the ball. It's hot, it's cold, it's dry, it's wet, the backboard's wood or it's metal, there's a chain net or a string net or no net. It just comes down to getting the ball through the hole. There are no intrusions. The Game, on the other hand, is rife with invasions by virtue of its very size and scope and facets, an extravaganza begging to be violated.

There is no bias in the game, no culture, no nationality, no politics. There is no race, no prejudice, no stereotype. You call your own fouls. The ball may be oblong, the hoop may be crooked, and the court may be slanted, but those items are endemic and they are the same for each player. You may be black and I may be white, and outside of the game that may weigh heavily in our respective opportunities and quality of life, but here, it's irrelevant, just like height. If I'm tall, you know you have to juke me to get to the rack or put me on my heels to create space for you to launch that jumper. It still comes down to you and me and the ball.

The Game is a lightning rod for intrusions of all sorts. The Olympic Games: the Munich Massacre of 1972, political boycotts in 1980 and 1984, and the bowed heads and raised,

7

black fists at Mexico City in 1968. Those fists were not used to punch an opponent or to gain a game advantage. They served as a political statement on a podium raised for its occupants by virtue of their performance in the game. Those fists, in fact, belonged not to John Carlos or to Tommy Smith; they belonged to a civil rights movement.

Time magnifies everything. Life thrives in bountiful waves of optimism even as decay eats away. In the 1950s, The Game was played out in small venues before limited audiences by skinny guys with horn-rimmed glasses in short shorts. There was no television and precious little press coverage. There was no fame, no glory, and there were no million-dollar contracts. The Game was little more than the game with a scoreboard and a clock. The Game and the game were virtually the same.

All of that has changed. The Game has grown from little more than a rumor into front-page news. Like Jack's beanstalk, The Game has twisted, expanded, and morphed, fueled by small town boredom, big city newspapers, opportunistic agents, college recruiters, professional scouts, national television, and international acclaim, all seeking and feeding off of money — contract money, play-off shares, recruiting money, endorsement money, sponsorship money. The first thought that crosses a parent's mind when little Johnny throws one in during a kindergarten youth league game is stardom and fame and millions and millions of dollars. While little Johnny raises his hands to savor that moment, and that feeling, others are already plotting its conversion into cold, hard cash.

The game spawned this, but it doesn't in any way resemble it. The game is little more than an aging, addled mother cowering in the shadows as what was once her bouncing baby bursts through its humble beginnings, a steroid-raged, power-hungry, self-glorifying, rule-breaking criminal now so grotesque and out of control that even its benefactors recoil in horror as search lights pan across the police helicopters and a voice through the bullhorn warns, "Give yourself up!" But it won't give itself up, not now. The players glance curiously and worriedly back at the game, which is powerless. The Game is a monster that will not obey.

The game found me, sidling up like another kid skipping rocks. Neighborhoods in the early 1960s abounded with games, from hopscotch and hide-and-seek to marbles and tag. It was a time before cable TV, video games, home computers, or the Internet. Entertainment was a choice between three channels of network TV or going outside to play. I was seven the first time I encountered a game of baseball at the lot across the street from our house. As with most addictions, it started slowly and simply, just a whiff of batting and fielding, neither of which I did well, though my interest was reinforced by the benevolence of the older kids who insisted I swing until I connected and who forgave my inability or unwillingness to get in front of hard ground balls.

The lot was a haven for kids, perhaps sixty feet across and a hundred and fifty feet long, a long stretch of grass and dirt and a few small trees toward the back. I don't remember anyone ever mowing it. I suppose we kept the grass beat down with our endless succession of seasonal games: baseball and football, mostly, plus long snowball wars in the winter. The only blight on this parcel was an ashen patch in one corner where folks would drop and burn trash. In the summer, it smoldered constantly and more than once we nurtured along those flames, lit a few sticks, and marched around like marauding soldiers until someone inadvertently dropped their makeshift torch into the dry grass, igniting a wildfire, resulting in more attention from grown-ups and the fire department than we could ever imagine or want again.

The games were a direct byproduct of the lot, woven into its shape, its terrain, and the various trees, shrubs, and sidewalks scattered along the perimeter. A baseball hit against the Burslem's house was a double; a tennis ball hit over the trees and into the street was a home run. Football was tackle across the center plot, but touch across the sidewalk or near the smoldering pit. The one time our water balloon fight escalated to buckets and hoses and into the Burslem house, there were no rules at all, not when it was Mrs. Burslem herself throwing full buckets across the kitchen at her son, Tom, and me.

That's how kids played back in the sixties. For me, those first baseball games at the cramped lot spawned pickup games all over our neighborhood and up at Tillman School when we weren't doing chores like mowing the lawn, raking leaves, or shoveling snow. My father was always upgrading our house. One year, he built a shed because we had no garage. I helped him secure the foundation, frame it, and nail up the walls. Despite its lack of windows and makeshift door, I had visions of a clubhouse, visions that quickly died once all the tools and supplies were crammed inside. I spent a lot of time in my clubhouse, but it wasn't the playtime I'd hoped for. We also spent nearly two years finishing the basement, transforming it from a cellar with a smooth, cement floor and rough, concrete walls (great for playing any game) into a wood-paneled, tiled, family room. The transformation was unfit for action, as the panels were prone to punctures from our sword fights and sections would cave in when we checked each other into the boards during hockey games.

At school, I would recruit guys to play after class, carefully choosing players to balance out the sides. On summer mornings, I'd be on the phone, lining up enough guys to play boundary ball or screen ball, baseball derivatives that we could play with as few as four players. And in later years, after I finally discovered hoop, on snowy, winter weekends I'd shovel the neighbor's driveway to clear space for basketball, since we had neither a paved driveway nor a hoop of our own.

Tillman School featured a couple of worn backstops with base paths carved into the dry grass. Sometimes there were other kids there playing and so we had to negotiate to create space for our game. If they were older boys, we chose our logic and our words very carefully. I don't remember getting beat up or even being physically threatened, but age had its privileges, a fact of which we were acutely aware. More than once we idled along one side of a field simply waiting for the older boys to tire of what they were doing. Sometimes we absorbed them into our game, usually without incident. Regardless, we worked it out.

11

Once the game began, we competed. We were constantly adjusting, compensating for lopsided advantages, and realigning to handle the arrival and departure of players. Oftentimes, the game would last for hours with players leaving and arriving such that nearly every player would change out, leaving just a few at the end who'd been there at the start. The game itself seemed a living organism, constantly adapting to its parts and the environment.

There was very little bragging or belittling back then because we always had an eye on the next game. Smack talk would have been a death toll in these games. In this way, we learned to even the sides and handicap the game because our future fun depended on it. We learned to compete for competition's sake, not just to win, and never to win big.

Those days were about neighborhood, brotherhood, and friendship. When we climbed on our bikes and headed out to play, it was just us and the other kids—no coaches, no officials, and no parents. If we got in a fight, we worked it out or pedaled home. There was no calling home to have a parent come pick you up; there was no orchestration of any kind, nothing to validate or prolong a disagreement. So the next day, we got up and went back out and played with those same kids, because yesterday was all but forgotten. It was symbiotic. Without the games, there was no competition. And without each other, there were no games.

There were no club teams when I was growing up, not for baseball or basketball, not for any sport. The Game had not yet spread its influence and greed to youth sports, so there was no impetus to practice one sport year-round, or to gain proficiency or an edge. There were youth leagues for baseball and football, in each of which I played, but those games were for fun, for friends to play and for parents to watch; otherwise, they were a secret. Today, parents rabidly press forward in bleacher seats and jockey for position among the other starry-eyed promoters. Back then, parents sat placidly in lawn chairs, swatting at boredom with mindless chatter like worthless hand waves against the flies. And that's if they attended at all. My parents showed at every game, lips drawn tight against the dust of the baseball diamonds, blankets pulled around them against the winter chill of football. Those teams were no big deal to me; neither were the uniforms or the games. Those teams just gave me a chance to play.

My first experience with The Game was the first basketball game I played for real. I was in ninth grade, the final year of junior high school. It was the first time I ever wore a basketball uniform, my first game with referees, and the first time anyone watched me play. A couple hundred fans watched that day and the most surprised of any of them must have been my father. For all the grounders he'd hit to me, for all the pitches he'd caught, and for all the football plays he'd seen me make, he had never seen me play hoop.

My father gave me a basketball for Christmas once, I think it was fifth or sixth grade. I don't know why. I'd never asked for one, never shown interest in the game, and never expressed wanting to play. It was a time before NBA games were televised, when college games were just a few lines on the

13

sports page. Maybe he saw that I would be tall and figured that basketball is what tall guys do, although he'd never played either. Or maybe he'd just run out of Christmas gift ideas.

We didn't have much money back then, and when I saw my new basketball, I noticed immediately that it was all orange—it had no black lines—and it was rubber like the bouncy, stretchy material used for kickballs. I was no expert, but I sensed that this basketball was low grade, a product of my father's ignorance of the game and modest income. But we were raised to covet our gifts and to show gratitude, so I thanked him profusely and carried the ball around the house with me for the next few days. And so, just a few days later, my father walked me up to Tillman for some hoop.

Having learned both baseball and football on a sandlot, I was able to bring the game home to my parents so that they could learn from my stories and eventually from my games. But as my father and I stood on the blacktop that day, we quickly realized that neither of us had a clue about basketball. We were all alone. We began heaving tentative shots up at the iron, net-less rim, clanging metal like a couple of blacksmiths. I wasn't particularly engaged until a couple of other kids, maybe a year or two older, arrived and began shooting on the other basket. At once, I became quite conscious of our ineptitude. I was also keenly aware of their black-striped, composite basketball, which produced a smart *slap* each time it hit the blacktop, a stark contrast to the *plong* my ball produced. I think my father sensed it too.

"Do you want to go play with them?" he asked. I didn't even need to look at his face to know this was a directive along the lines of, "How about you rake the leaves." I knew who these kids were, but I didn't know them. I was younger, had no sense of the rules, and certainly didn't possess the skills to participate. On top of it all, I was painfully shy. So, sure, Dad. They surely had no interest in including me, but they felt the presence and impetus of a parent, which back in the sixties was an omnipotent force. And so we played. I don't remember the game or how long I played with them. I remember feeling lost, and when I discovered that my father had left, I felt abandoned. He did leave my ball there, sitting in the grass, bouncy and stripe-less.

The game flourished in our neighborhood, buoyed by the seasons, fresh and clean among the budding spring maples, lush and green as the lawns in summer, and crisp as the autumn winds. Baseball, football, and basketball thrived along with dozens of derivatives crafted by the interests and abilities of its players. The months crept along and the neighborhood kids began to grow up and the game remained true to us and our innocence, carefully handicapped to maintain interest and competition. The game permeated the neighbors and the neighborhood, my little brother and I playing slow-motion football games, tackle affairs in which we could writhe and twist and pound each other without getting hurt. Mom would always holler from the kitchen ten minutes before dinnertime and the next play would last the entire time, an endless succession of fumbles snatched and run back, and then caught and dropped and fumbled again, until her final call for dinner when whoever had the ball would find daylight to score the game-winning touchdown.

We played epic hockey games in our basement on winter nights after dinner and homework. Once the basement was tiled and paneled, we'd scoot up and down in our socks, using yardsticks and a wiffle ball since our hockey sticks and pucks were way too threatening to Dad's monument to hard work and perseverance. We'd race ahead and execute hip checks and prolonged slides across the floor, more than once cracking the panels or peeling off the cheap, rubber floor molding. I think about him now, our father sitting upstairs, reading his paper and listening to his two sons tearing up his basement. I suppose he'd envisioned sitting down there watching TV, sipping coffee, his brood gathered around like pups at the foot of their master, but I also imagine it was a fair trade. We were good kids engaged in healthy fun under his roof. The game had come home to roost.

Eventually, Dad bought a Ping-Pong table and placed it at one end of the basement. If he'd thought that doing so would curtail the hockey, he was sorely mistaken. We engaged that table as a pair of defensemen to be skirted, or slid under and our games continued. But that table became the sole venue where Dad let down his hair and played with us. When I was in high school, he and I were pretty evenly matched my windmill slam versus his skilled defense and a determination that bordered on desperation. The game created a bond, a union not especially common between a father and his teenage son. My father began to track our wins with pencil marks on the kitchen bulletin board, and by the time I left for college, the hash marks ran the

16

length of the board, top to bottom, and numbered in the hundreds. I think I owned a few more marks than he by then, and I imagine he stared at that simple monument to the game more than once over quiet, staid dinners when I was gone.

And then there was wiffle ball, a two-man confrontation of pitch and hit with nothing extraneous, no fielders, no base runners, simply a field with defined boundaries and designated hits according to where and how far one hit the ball. Our game borrowed from several iterations I'd seen or played, from the wooden corkball bat introduced by Albert Roos, to the outfield fence along Bernice Avenue that Jim Becker established years before.

My brother and I were teenagers by then. We parlayed our childhood years of sharing a bedroom, a bathroom, a bath tub (until we'd grown so tall that our legs intertwined and Mom abandoned efficiency for a little privacy, thank you very much), the back of the station wagon on long vacation drives, a portable television, unwanted food passed under the table, and a thousand other details growing up in our tiny house. We rolled all of that up into a game of complete and utter cooperation, in which the play so far outstripped the outcome that the feel of the bat in our hands seemed like just about the best feeling in life— at least, up to that point in our lives.

I lugged that corkball bat up from Albert's and stood in our side yard as the entire playing field emerged before my eyes: home plate carved out against the chimney next to a hedge, foul lines defined by two bushes, one in each corner of the yard, the pitching spot between the street and the sidewalk, and an

17

outfield extending across the street to the Tilden's yard, house, and fenced play area. It felt like a jailbreak each time we emerged, twin renegades gobbling up the neighborhood, pounding that ball, raining shots up and down the street, but mostly into the Tilden's yard, up against their house, slapping against their windows and onto their paved play area, the swing set, the plastic playhouse where their toddler must have cowered in fear at the size and impertinence of those crazed savages, who should have known better but continued to run and revel and ravage and the Tildens thinking, "Even when we gathered up and kept their wiffle balls, they continued to produce more. One even found its way right through our station wagon window, and the only reason they didn't retrieve that one was because we were backing out of the driveway at the time!"

I'd stand at home plate and settle into my left-handed hitting stance, notable because it forced my brother, Mitch, to develop pitches that broke away, no minor feat for a right-handed pitcher. But he did it, he created an arsenal of breaking stuff including one wrist-breaker that started up and in and then dive-bombed low and away. Knowing full well I couldn't catch it, I'd swing anyway, a giant swoop of the bat that carried me back into the hedge where the bat remained wedged as I writhed and flexed my wrist in pain. Even if I'd known of the arthritis I was inflicting on my future self, I would have stayed my course because adulthood was no more than a myth while the game was real and pervasive and completely intoxicating. I'd settle into my stance and stare out at my kid brother, framed by two

18

maple trees and a background so lush and green (and about to be violated yet again) that I'd drift into a calm contentment, a virtual coma of indifference and satisfaction knowing that he had to bring one in for a strike, wondering which law-of-physics-defying pitch he'd summon, and trusting that if I let it go, he'd call it honestly, ball or strike. But I was sure that if it came close, I was gonna take a hack, and even if I didn't drive it into the trees or possibly into the Tilden's play area, there'd be another one and another one after that.

We kept score only because the games had to have a start and an end. Those scores, though, were incidental, as were balls and strikes. What defined those games were the plays, sneaking an inside slider by the other guy, or lunging to pick a fly ball out of the trees as it pinballed among the branches, or the feel of connecting and driving that bad boy deep into the Tilden's front yard where nobody would track it down. Each and every play was immortalized by my nonstop, top-of-my-lungs radio announcer's voice, which carried so well and so often that Mr. Andrews, at the dinner table half a block away, would calmly put down his paper, glance at his sons, and observe, "Well, it sounds like Drew's winning." Anticipation of those games got me through the long, sweaty hours working a summer job in a fetid shoe warehouse. Our games served as Mitch's inspiration to mow the foul lines and field into the side yard. Home from my summer job, I'd bound out to meet him and we'd race around shirtless in the ninety degree heat and 80 percent humidity, finally answering Mom's summons to dinner, sweating over a casserole, gulping milk by the gallon, itching to get back outside before the sweat had dried on our backs.

Our worlds, our existence, already compressed by the innocence and anticipation of youth, further shrank into that side yard to the near exclusion and disregard of anything else. We'd formed a mini biosphere, self-contained with ample water through the rubber hose at the side of the house, snacks in the fridge just a short jaunt away, and spare windows in the basement to replace those we broke with errant pitches and throws. We felt impervious to the elements, playing through heat, humidity, rain, and sometimes snow, showing no regard for any diversion—except for Cindy Kunz, who at seventeen rode past on her bike in a bikini and gym shorts. She was in full blossom and who were we to trample such a flower after having laid to waste all the other flora and fauna the neighborhood had to offer so that after impulsive dashes between cars and lightning fast raids on the Tilden's bushes to retrieve balls, after racing headlong for months and months we finally, just that one time, paused to marvel at nature's bounty, to exchange a few words and steal more than a few glances such that although she didn't exactly change the game, Cindy at least impacted it and grateful were we that the game had drawn us out into the yard that day and at that precise time so that we could experience all that life and puberty had to offer.

The game is a thread, microscopic in breadth, a hint of gossamer drawing unsuspecting souls together in simple competition to the exclusion of all else, from a mother and her infant playing peekaboo to two old men hunched over a

20

chessboard and everything in between. The game unifies, joining father and son pitching baseballs at night after a long day at the office, pitches pounding the mitt or skipping past, one time even knocking the coffee cup handle clean off and the boy scampering off to retrieve a wild one as the dad sips and ponders. The game allows brothers to bond even when the age gap is too great for real competition, their mutual effort to fashion a bridge between disparate age and ability forming a bond of trust and respect. And finally, it is the game's presence and past and its memory that inspires each of us to forgive time and aging and their inevitable accompanying attrition because the gray and hobbled old man before me was once lean and powerful and magnificent and some of what became of him was due to the investment he made in me and after all the batting practice he threw and grounders he hit, his shoulder aches and his knees need replacement. Even though youth masks it so you don't realize it all when you're a kid, someday it happens to you and suddenly you realize you are him and you are left wishing you could go back and tell him what you now know and perhaps thank him for what he gave up. You imagine him back then receiving nothing in return except the knowledge that you would someday understand but he could not hasten that day or that revelation and he abided it all so graciously knowing that your realization might be too late for him. So you console yourself that in the absence of your gratitude he clung to hope and conviction and the future. Turn the page and you find yourself staring out at the new generation and you wince as his pitches bruise your palm and crack your thumb and realize that today

21

the game is growth and achievement and tomorrow it will be love and memories. The game is a gift.

Just a thread, nearly invisible, and you wonder how anything so fine could reach so far and tie so tightly, tight enough to survive all the human frailties and insecurities that divide us. These were the midsixties and we followed the game, roaming the fenceless backyards, cavorting in and out of each other's houses, oblivious to the nightly newscasts that diligently documented the black and white images of Vietnam, of the Communist scare and the race riots. That's the way it was in our neighborhood, a several block radius from Tillman Elementary School. Across town, quite literally across the railroad tracks, the same games were played; the same relationships were developing on the same type of schoolyards with the same limited resources. There was only one difference: we were white and they were black.

Chapter 2

There has never been any black and white with Mr. Miller, at least not in a racial sense. To him, black and white are simple distinctions between entities or integers. He scrawls across the blackboard in typical math teacher cadence—the clack clack clack *of chalk on board—listing the numbers for the five Raytown South starters like he's drawing up a math problem. Their numbers are all we know since we've never seen them play and have never heard or read a thing about them. We scouted Northwest High all year as they ran off twenty-one in a row in the Public High League. We went to see them play and read about them in the* Post-Dispatch *sports section. We knew each of their starters, their height, weight, number, and their strengths and weaknesses. We even knew their nicknames. Our entire scouting report on Raytown South, on the other hand, consists of what Mr. Miller saw watching the other semifinal game yesterday afternoon. Unlike most Final Fours in which the semifinal games are played back-to-back while players sit in the stands watching the other game, the Raytown semifinal was moved from evening to afternoon. They were playing yet another all-black team, Sumner High from St. Louis, and officials wanted that game played in the daytime just in case. And so we stayed in our hotel rooms, napping like kindergartners on their blankets.*

Billy and I figured Sumner would win, but we were relieved to hear they didn't. They have some great athletes along with that inner city soul mystique. We heard Ed Stolle scored forty-one for Raytown South, but we're not worried. Stolle is the Raytown South center, which means I'll guard him. The only player who's given me any trouble this year was Ruben Shelton of Northwest, but he was fast and strong and black. Stolle's a skinny white guy, at least that's what someone told me. I'll handle him and that'll inspire my guys while demoralizing theirs. I look up at Mr. Miller then at the blackboard.

"Stolle is 43. Williams, you've got him." Mr. Miller's voice is gravelly and gruff, like Mr. Potter in the movie It's a Wonderful Life. *"Rogers, you'll guard 52. Moulder, you take 22." Wait, go back to Stolle. Robert's got him? I glance over. Rock's just staring at the floor. He's got Stolle? "Stolle's handy around the basket, Robert. Deny him the ball, and if he does get it, stay on your feet. Don't try to block his shot." I smile. I used to try to block them all, especially last year. Then we played Parkway West and they had a six-foot-eight-inch big man, Ed Probst, and Mr. Miller was adamant before the game: don't try to block his shot. And of course, that was like telling a small child, "Don't open that box." So the first chance I got I went after Probst and packed him clean, a total roof job, so that I nearly dislocated his shoulder cramming the ball back down his arm. I was running down court and I couldn't look over because I knew Mr. Miller was furious, but what the hell. And then, tie game, less than a minute to go, and Probst lines up another one, same spot, and I have it planned. I'm going to pack him and grab it and go the other way and win it. So up he goes and here I come, and I get a lot of ball and just a little arm and they call the foul. He hits two free throws and we lose. There was no avoiding Mr.*

24

Miller's wrath after that. So let's hope Rock's listening to Mr. Miller better than I did. Stolle's the only number with a name, with an identity. The other four are just uniform numbers, faceless and anonymous.

Tonight is it. There's no other chance, no foul in the act, no two extra ticks on the clock. Win or lose, tonight's it. Somewhere tomorrow, some kid will be shooting in the dusk at a tilted rim with a mangled net as the clock ticks down, five…four…three…he shoots…he misses it…but he was fouled. He goes to the line, one to tie and two to win…to beat…Kirkwood High and Drew Rogers…because that's the game he saw tonight…

Mr. Miller details our zone presses, when we'll use them and what we'll fall back into. He chooses a passive press for starters and again, I'm nettled. Let's throw our 1–2–1–1 full court job at them, the one where Jesse presses up and Robert picks off the desperation heaves. But Coach has seen them. Does he doubt our ability to pressure them into mistakes? After the havoc we wreaked all year?

Coach Mansinger sticks his head in the door, the roar of the crowd outside entering with him. It's the loudest crowd I've heard. Is it the acoustics of this old barn? I think there were more people at the Northwest game, but the crowd here's a lot louder. "Raytown! Raytown! Raytown!" It's them. I smile to myself. Gonna be a lot of disappointed Kansas City hayseeds tonight.

"Two minutes!" Mr. Mansinger looks disheveled. Not like the Northwest game when a huge black guy spit right in his face as we struggled through the half time crowd back onto the court. That night, he kept walking, staring straight ahead, and let that goo just run down

his cheek not deigning a glance or a confrontation. Tonight he looks charged, his hair standing up as if from static electricity.

"OK, gather 'round." We stand and push in toward Mr. Miller for our minute of silent prayer. Mine is always the same: "God, thank you for your gifts and for bringing me here right now. Please make this a fairly-played game with no injuries and no bad calls. Make the better team win." I know better than to ask for a win or any other direct help from upstairs. Jim Morrison's lyric echoes silently in my mind: "You cannot petition the Lord with prayer." So, I'm not. I'm just saying let the better team win. We've been the better team all year.

That's it. No pep talk, no final words of wisdom. Mr. Miller coaches teams in practice and ingrains in their souls what to do and how to do it. With a team like ours, that's enough. Everyone knows what we're going to do, so good luck stopping us. Thirty-one teams have tried and thirty-one have died. Raytown's number thirty-two. But out of nowhere, Mr. Miller says something about not shooting unless we know we can make it and then shooting a lot. What? He steps aside and we line up, shortest to tallest, and then out we go with Tommy Grice in the lead. We walk between the bleachers on what's left of a cinder track. Brewer Fieldhouse. They run indoor track here. Perfect. We'll turn this game into a track meet and run them off the floor like always. We pause for a moment at the foot of the raised floor, and I get my first real look at the crowd. It's all red and white—Kirkwood colors—but it's not really Kirkwood red. It's a brighter red, a Raytown red. Tommy hops up on the floor and the rest of us follow. The wood is old and soft and bouncy. I remember it from my recruiting trip. You get good air jumping off of it and it's easy on the knees. We circle the floor once as the Kirkwood fans whoop it up, and then we race down the

26

center of the floor to leap and touch the backboard in succession. Tommy's the shortest, but he's got hops. He grabs the rim. At five feet eight inches, it's an impressive feat and we think it intimidates the other team. But Raytown's not even out there yet, so they're spared the sight of such raw athleticism.

And then they emerge. I don't see them, but their crowd is so loud. It's the only time all year that our crowd has been out-roared or "out-reded." Maybe they think they can win. Too bad. We run layup lines for a few minutes and then go into the Kirkwood weave. Three players across midcourt and three on the baseline as the ball whips around and we sprint and soar in for layups or pull up for jumpers. Our crowd knows it, exalts it, and this is when other teams start stealing glances to catch a glimpse of us, our awe, our mystique. We're athletic and fast and the ball is a blur.

Raytown's starting five is watching. In fact, they've quit warming up and stand next to their coach. He stares, studious and unfazed, pointing at us as his team nods. I look straight at them and they don't look away. Their coach says something to Stolle, who nods and then trots back to their layup line.

The clock ticks down inside of four minutes and we seven regulars shoot while the rest of the team rebounds and kicks them back out. I get a chance to scan the crowd to find my parents and my brother. It's tough tonight because it's so packed, and I never want to seem like I'm looking in case they were to stand up and wave. Plus, with all the red and white—Raytown's red and white—and there's more of them than us. I end up not finding my family. And it's so loud...

27

The lights dim and the crowd settles for the national anthem. This is my eighty-sixth varsity hoop game, yet I never fail to marvel at this moment. I glance around at the crowd, up at the flag, and then into the darkness behind the bleachers, and bask in the moment. I'm about to play a game that I love. Thank you for all of this. The announcer introduces the starting lineups. There's never any order to it, like starting with the guards or some such approach. Tonight, it goes Robert and Jesse, then me, and then the guards. Billy's last. We pull together, the five of us at the free throw line. Our wool warm-up jackets are unsnapped and hang loosely over our worn, red uniforms with the tiny numbers. Raytown's got nice, new, white uniforms with red trim and big numbers. They're staring at us again and murmuring amongst themselves.

We gather around Mr. Miller, the reserves pack in around us, and Mr. Miller has to shout to be heard. Something about which of them to spot in our zone. I can't really hear him, but I'm figuring I'm gonna cheat off of 52 to help out on Stolle. I'm thinking Stolle's gonna need someone cheating over to help out on me or I'll light him up, and Billy's going to penetrate, and Tommy's going to run out on them and—hell, let's get going.

We walk on the court and the noise is just deafening. I've never been in the center of anything this loud. It's not unsettling, but it is peculiar, especially since there's more of them than us, and that's never happened. Our fans have never been drowned out, but that's exactly what's happening right now. I stand in the center circle with Stolle, and he's just this lanky, goofy-looking beanpole with a nervous grin and a crooked haircut. I'm thinking, "How the hell did he light Sumner up like that?" Stolle rubs his hands on his shorts, and I figure

28

he's nervous, then he looks straight up in the air like he's hearing the crowd for the first time and he's beckoning them, and it's so loud it's like a huge tarp spreading over us, slowly settling down on us, compressing the air and compacting the court, just refusing to be ignored. Stolle nods because it's energizing him and I don't know what it's doing to us except that when I look around at my guys, nobody's looking back and that's the first tiny indication that we're not exactly all together right now; that crowd and that noise have fractured us just a little and Stolle wipes his hands on his shorts one last time, and suddenly I realize he's not nervous, he's just going to work.

Sugar Bear

Now I could understand your tears and your shame,
She called you "boy" instead of your name.
When she wouldn't let you inside,
When she turned and said,
"But honey, he's not our kind."
                    –"Society's Child," Janis Ian

Being black in the midsixties was far different from being black today. Despite the Fifteenth Amendment's mandate of the right to vote for all US citizens, many southern states continued to block blacks from voting through literacy tests and poll taxes. Discriminatory acts were widespread throughout the northern states as well. It was a time before hip hop, baggy basketball shorts, Michael Jordan, or Barrack Obama. Any hope for a black president was stymied by the simple fact that so many blacks were not even allowed to vote. Black recording artists were largely limited to the Motown genre with lyrics that were a far cry from present day rap. There was absolutely no tolerance for cries to kill a cop or any white person. Black actors appeared only in supporting roles. The 1968 TV show *Julia* was one of the first weekly series to depict a black woman in a non-stereotypical role. There were no endorsement contracts for black athletes. It was a time of suppression and prejudice. Though the race riots captured the nation's attention throughout the sixties, the nagging issues that spurred violence were mostly unknown or ignored by white America. Blacks in and around Kirkwood were subject to taunts, threats, and aggression, with the knowledge that they might receive no support from local police and would likely find no safe haven outside of their own neighborhoods. It was neither hip to be black nor cool to associate with them.

Change was afoot, though. Congress took steps at the legislative level by passing both the Civil Rights Act of 1964, which barred discrimination in employment or public accommodations, and the Voting Rights Act of 1965, which prohibited states from imposing qualifications that limited an individual's right and ability to vote. It wasn't until 1967 that the Supreme Court ruled that prohibiting interracial marriage was unconstitutional, forcing sixteen states to revise their laws. These acts were far less newsworthy than the riots, especially to kids, so when I graduated from my all-white elementary school to my 99 percent white junior high school, such legislation was less than muted. It was invisible.

Society was changing, too. A series of jolts and storms arose, much more caustic than legislation. In 1966, the Black Panthers formed. A year later, Stokely Carmichael coined the term "Black Power." In a speech, he summoned black people "to fight for their liberation by any means necessary," calling on them to become armed and ready to fight the Ku Klux Klan. Then, in April of 1968, Dr. Martin Luther King was shot dead by a white man, triggering riots in Baltimore, DC, Chicago, and New York City. As a fourteen-year-old kid, my first reaction was to duck away from the intrusion of these events, from this reality thrust upon my sheltered life.

My impression of blacks in general stemmed from what I'd learned in history courses: slavery, poverty, poor education, and limited opportunity. *Segregation* was a vocabulary word, its definition to be memorized, but never understood. Closer to home, my rare encounters with black children were uneventful, from the dozen or so black kids I met through a one-week church school course, to the one or two I met in junior high. I was too naïve to associate them or their lives with televised race riots, or legislation that was thousands of miles away, or even the ghettos that my family occasionally skirted in the car. I knew only that black kids had it a lot tougher than white kids. And when I began to meet and befriend black teammates, I found their plight to be a source of discomfort and embarrassment, a wedge between us imposed by a history of prejudice and a society defined by and still propagating separation and discrimination.

At a time when black athletes were just beginning to break down barriers in college and in professional sports, a platform that could have been a melting pot for all races was instead fraught with distrust and bias. Professional football featured no blacks as quarterbacks, as teams appeared convinced that the position was too cerebral. Major League Baseball maintained a similar bias with respect to black pitchers, only a handful of whom were allowed to play that position. The old American Football League had survived its early struggles to compete with the NFL and was beginning to flourish, partly due to its openness to black athletes. But in January of 1965, its scheduled All-Star game had to be moved from New Orleans to Houston after numerous instances in which black players were refused service by hotels and businesses, and white cab drivers refused to carry black passengers. The white players supported the black players by boycotting New Orleans, but it must have been an uneasy alliance. I would soon learn of the challenges that come with befriending black teammates in the face of society's constant and insistent intrusions.

Jesse Jackson was an open book. He was utterly without guile. Of the Kirkwood High starting five my senior season, Jesse was the first I'd played with previously. We'd been teammates on a baseball team, not basketball. I'd played five years of recreational league baseball, and by the time I was thirteen, many players were drifting away. Some of the coaches saw an opportunity and a need to combine the remaining, more serious players into more competitive teams. This was before club teams and leagues, so there was no established venue for players who wanted to raise their game. And into this void stepped Roger Burnett, a former college baseball player and the father of Tommy Burnett, star pitcher and shortstop for the Mustangs.

I had lost to the Mustangs for five years. Their players included brothers Keith and Paul Bambie as well as speedy outfielder Andre Williams and catcher Kirk Johnson, who were more athletic than my Westover Greenies. They were also extremely well coached, thanks to Mr. Burnett, who turned out to be an excellent recruiter as well. Mr. Burnett reached into the Greenies team just as it was falling victim to the varied interests and opportunities of junior high school. Burnett plucked four of us to join his core group, the sum of which he moved up to play against teams whose players were a year older.

The result was not exactly the Dream Team. The four newcomers donned the worn and ragged, Mustang uniforms, and ventured out onto the sun-dried, hard pack of dusty Marshall Field in the sunken delta next to the Meramec River. Spring downpours softened the turf to putty into which we carved footprints that the summer sun then baked into hardened ridges and gullies. These produced catastrophic bad hops and torn knees when sliding. And those were the good conditions. Once summer had burned away the grass and dried up the spring rainfall the infield was coated in a thick carpet of dust, which hid the nooks and crannies and occasionally absorbed a grounder entirely as though a gopher had reached up and yanked the ball into its hole. It was like playing on the moon.

Day games sweltered, lacking any breeze, such that even from a seat in the dugout we would sweat through the cheap, cotton uniforms adding one more challenge to play: swinging a bat in the scratchy, clinging, constricting uniform shirt, now several salty pounds heavier and scented like a sulfur mine. It was a recipe for misery. Take one cotton uniform, add salt, then mix in several helpings of snow cone in cherry, grape, orange, or perhaps one of each flavor. Heat to a boil so that the ice melts between bites, and then run the colored syrup down the arms, across the sleeves, and splash onto the chest, and voilà: steamed teenager soup. Evening games provided a small respite from the heat, by five or ten degrees perhaps, but the humidity climbed along with the mosquitoes, mythically huge, winged beasts, rising from the banks of the Meramec, ominously approaching the fields like helicopters on a raid. They devoured bare arms and legs like locusts across a field of flesh. Clouds of gnats offered air cover such that when waving a free hand to create a sight line to the batter, the mosquitoes would sneak in and ravage one's arms or neck. I had never lived anywhere else, and so I abided these monstrosities of nature, lying in bed at night, scratching the bites, and starving for a cool breeze through the open windows of our air-conditioned-less house.

This suburb of St. Louis, this gateway to the West, had actually been sought out by settlers through arduous journeys from the East. They had stopped, looked around, and spying an attractive parcel (as best they could through the gnats and mosquitoes), they had actively chosen to set up house. I imagine my ancestors' wagon train rattling along, somehow crossing the

34

Mississippi, its leader, the intrepid Bullmoose Rogers, raising his hand to halt the crusade, turning, rising in his saddle, and issuing forth in a booming voice the words both inspirational and prophetic. "This'll do."

In so doing, my forefathers brought further meaning to the term *settler*, forgoing the trip to what is now Southern California to languish in a bug-infested sauna. This left my generation to sweat it out while those who didn't settle until they reached paradise bestowed on their descendants a Mediterranean climate, beach volleyball, surfing, and girls in bikinis, a culture with which we were only passingly familiar thanks to the meager scraps tossed our way in the form of Beach Boys albums and Annette Funicello beach blanket movies.

In the meantime, the thirteen-year-old Mustangs joined the older teams, and managed to win half of their games thanks to good talent across the roster. We lacked in star power, however, which each of the older teams possessed. From Randy Scott, who consistently found the cornfield with towering drives that disappeared among the gnats only to land with a crunch ten rows deep in the corn, to Jim Menner, a broad-shouldered lefty pitcher with an overpowering fastball and a bevy of cute girlfriends stationed behind the backstop who made whiffing a particularly painful event as each time we trudged back to the dugout, his entourage jumped and celebrated Menner's mastery and with it our humiliation.

That's not to say that the Mustangs were devoid of character—or characters. Keith Bambi was a batting practice icon. He swatted continuously at pitch after pitch until he'd launch one and then interrupt things with a brazen homerun trot, leaving the batting practice pitcher to wait, hands on hips, as Keith circled the bases. He practiced signing autographs in anticipation of baseball greatness, which, though never quite realized, proved incentive enough to master a beautiful writing hand and a boundless variety of Ks and Bs. Keith's brother, Paul, would compose songs or alter popular songs about opposing teams, singing from his second base position over to Keith at third base and me at shortstop, more than once forcing us to field a grounder while bent over in laughter.

The other teams were none too thrilled to play the Mustangs since we were younger. They teased us before and after games, along with displaying occasional intimidation tactics like spiking us when sliding into base. We drew the line at brushback pitches, however. I'd read about old time baseball hitters fighting back against headhunting pitchers. They'd bunt down the first base line, forcing the pitcher to field the ball, and then run the pitcher over. I tried this tactic once, though it fizzled out when my perfectly placed bunt rolled to a stop halfway up the line with the pitcher still standing on the mound and me slowing my race to first base to wait for him to arrive. I found myself standing over that ball and glaring at the inert pitcher as he watched the first baseman swoop in, field the ball, and tag me out. Keith, on the other hand, left nothing to chance. Whenever a pitch came anywhere near his head, he'd mysteriously lose his grip when swinging at the next pitch and his bat would come pinwheeling back at the pitcher. Keith would stare at his open palms and then vigorously rub them on his uniform while shaking his head and hollering an unctuous, "Sorry!" to the properly disciplined pitcher.

So the following season, Mr. Burnett upgraded again. As a few of the less interested Mustangs wandered off, Jesse Jackson showed up. I had no idea where he came from or who he was, but he provided instant star power to the Mustangs, and in so doing, he elevated us from the middle of the pack to dominance. Jackson was a dark-skinned black player who, even at age fourteen, had muscles, athleticism, and skill. And he had presence. A catcher, Jackson was a ubiquitous presence behind the plate, bouncing around, fielding, and blocking pitches. He'd holler encouragement and confidence to his team and his pitcher while maintaining a steady stream of consciousness with the hitter, down in his crouch, sliding out to block a pitch, bouncing up to gun it back to the pitcher, then leaping up to throw out would-be stealers. "That's it, that's it, baby. Same thing, this one. You got this guy. He ain't even wanting none of you. Don't be looking down here. Even if you know what's coming, you're not gonna hit it. And over there on first base, don't you even think about stealing because I got you, too."

And with a bat in his hands Jesse was a marauder. His drives found the cornfield on a line, sizzling as though they'd wipe out gnats like an electronic bug zapper—*pop, pop, pop*. He had fast hands and strong forearms, and most of his hot shots went right back at the pitcher creating the impression that he aimed not just to win, but to gather scalps as well, intending to keep a collection of battered and demoralized pitchers around his belt. Jackson ran upright, his legs turning like wheels, leaning

37

in just slightly as he rounded first to stretch a gapper into a double, the infielders casting nervous glances behind them. They'd try to track the incoming throw while maneuvering out of Jesse's path lest he run roughshod right over them. Jesse was seven innings of non-stop, uncompromising confidence, performance, and dominance.

We were a small group, numbering eleven total, with Jesse joining Andre as one of only two blacks. Nobody thought differently of them, at least not that I knew of, and to me, Jesse was simply a player, one who had helped elevate and transform our pack into a successful, high-level team. He was confident, outgoing, exuberant, and a great teammate. Through his first season with the Mustangs, Jackson appeared no different from me; we were just two athletes, two baseball players safe between the lines, unified in a quest to grow and win, to revel and cavort in the game. The smattering of parents, players, coaches from other teams, umpires, and concessionaires did not intrude. We remained safe within the game and we seemed virtually the same. At a time when race riots ignited across the United States and would continue to flare up throughout the sixties, baseball offered a safe venue, devoid of race and without bias or prejudice. To me, the cities of Baltimore, DC, and New York were family vacation destinations even when they made front-page news due to the riots. I'd see the television images of burning buildings, overturned cars, and looters running amok, and it all seemed so far away, like a dream or a rumor, just out of my sight line and whispering just beneath my consciousness. I figured Jesse must be the same way.

But he was not. He was different. The difference lay not in the color of his skin or the neighborhood in which he lived or in his family or his upbringing or anything one could point to in his life. The difference was what he had experienced, or to be accurate, to what I suppose he must have experienced. I was never privy to what growing up black in the sixties did to a person, how it marked or scarred or forced itself into one's state of mind, affecting where you went, who you went with, and what you did. I saw a public restroom marked *Colored* once in my life, and so it was just a novelty, an anachronism, a symbol of Southern racism broken loose and wandering, come to rest in a train station in Princeton, Illinois. It was just a door, just a sign, behind which I had no concept of or interest in what could be found inside.

But somebody built that restroom. They built one for men and one for women, and then they took the time to build that third restroom, to create that sign meant to channel black people there, to segregate them from whites, to judge and insult them. That was one room, one time for me. But for Jesse Jackson, things like that must have been constant and insistent, flashing out at him whenever he walked to school or ate out with his family. All it took, among the students and parents or fellow diners, all it took was one slight, however subtle, a stare, a sideways glance, a whisper, or even a wink, and then the galvanization felt by his mom or his friend or his teacher. They'd ignore the vibe or turn away or gloss over it, as each and every such affirmation would validate the act such that as a young boy, he learned that whites are that way. That's just how society

39

is, and dammit, young blood, that's who you are and where you stand.

Wherever those slights resided, it was deep inside because the open book that was Jesse was a sweet, simple read. In all of his transparency, I never saw a reflection of the racism that had woven itself inside, never a hint. Jesse Jackson had no agenda. Left to himself, he was maturing into a balanced, centered, confident young man. He was joyful, engaging, funny, and kind, like a little kid offering a freshly picked flower oblivious to the fuming gardener behind him. Jackson was a Sugar Bear, so I had no inkling of what he abided because he took no issue with it. He was as happy in his myopia as I was in my ignorance. But the riots were spreading and racism was resolute and pervasive. When the Mustangs traveled to rural Missouri, I caught a glimpse of racism through Jesse's eyes and it startled me.

The Mustangs had improved. We won our league that spring, beating the older teams thanks to Jesse's brilliance and our collective personal growth, and so Mr. Burnett wanted to push the envelope. At least that's what I figured when he announced that the Mustangs were scheduled to play several games in southern Missouri. Road trip!

Mr. Burnett added some pitching for the trip, including Menner (he of the man's body and attentive harem) and Dave Reiter, one of the older kids whose stuff had continued to baffle us, especially his sharp-breaking curve ball. These two older players not only rounded out our pitching staff, they changed the dynamics of our team. Reiter was sixteen and had a driver's

40

license. Menner was not yet sixteen, but he routinely took his folks' car out for a spin. These boys instantly became the prototypical bad influences, leading us on surreptitious quests for alcohol and girls, neither of which the rest of us knew what to do with, but both of which drew us irresistibly into the adventure.

A dozen players piled into three cars driven by Mr. Burnett and our two coaches. We headed south into the Ozark Mountains, the cars bobbing over an endless succession of hills such that when I looked back a few hours in, civilization as I knew it had disappeared, replaced by solid walls of pine and oak trees, sprawling up the hillsides and down the valleys as far as the eye could see. I'd been along this way before, once when Dad had scraped together enough money for a family vacation to Lake of the Ozarks, three days of cabin living, along with a boat rental, water skis, and the patience to get all three kids upright and around the lake a few turns. But that had been different. We'd pushed through to the resort in one shot, ordered to use the bathroom before since we would not stop to go and would not stop for a soda even though Drew and Mitch loudly identified every soda machine at every gas station in passing, but most of all we would not stop at Meramec Caverns or Onondaga Cave despite the never-ending billboards that fluttered by as we raced along, like rifling through the pages in a book.

This time, I was in a car with three other Mustangs including Jesse. The pace was leisurely and the other cars were nowhere to be seen. It was just the four of us wandering into a remote restaurant in the late afternoon while our driver, Mr. Johnson, drove across the two-lane highway to the gas station. It took a moment for our eyes to adjust to the darkened room where two old men seemed to materialize in the corner from out of nowhere. I stared over the cashier counter at the menu carved into wooden signs, licking my lips at the list of barbecued items, inhaling their rich scent from the kitchen. The two men stepped behind the counter and I heard one offer to take our order, but I was still staring at that menu. One of our players headed for the restroom and another sat at a table by the door, leaving Jesse and me at the counter.

"What's yours?" The man must have been sixty and he stared at me with his one good eye because the other one was closed tight. He looked like he was wincing from a bee sting, except one eventually opens their eye after a sting, and this eye would never open again, a certainty I felt happy with since I didn't care to see what lay beneath. I noticed as the other guy, just as old, took a seat on a stool at the end of the counter. He sat just looking at us. I ordered a sandwich and stepped aside so that Jesse could order, but the man turned to place my order with the cook, and then walked away to sit with his partner. Then the two of them just stared at us—or rather, they stared at Jesse, who turned and headed for the door. I caught Jesse outside, and before I could say anything, he grabbed my arm.

"Those two look like they ain't never even seen a colored boy." He looked at me with wide eyes. "Ever."

"They're just a couple of old guys," I said dismissively.

"Maybe so, but just get your food and let's go."

42

I asked him if he wanted something, but he quickly waved me off.

"Jesse, those two aren't anything to worry about. You could kick either of their butts."

But Jesse had turned and walked to the road, waiting for cars to pass, and then trotted across toward our car. As I watched him retreat, I tried to get my mind around what would make a big, strong black kid run from two old buzzards. Jesse had three of us with him plus Coach Johnson. But I couldn't picture the scene through his eyes, only through mine. To me, it was just some middle-of-nowhere pause in the road to gas up, grab a bite, and maybe hit the head. I could tell that Jesse saw it differently, and I knew that was because he was black.

The few times I'd ridden through a ghetto or ventured into a group of black kids at Kirkwood Park, I'd been the scared one. Watching film of the race riots in Detroit and DC, I saw the blacks as the aggressors; they were the ones to be feared. I didn't fear Jesse because he was my friend and teammate, but I figured he could whip me in a fight, just as he could whip those two old hillbillies. What I had yet to comprehend was that Jesse was a minority, a very visible minority, one that had been targeted and banished by the majority, by white people. And some of those white people were hateful and vindictive, and some even donned white robes and burned crosses. The more stupid and more isolated a white person was, the closer to the hate mongers they were likely to be, and so, as each hill pulled the rest of us out into the boonies, it pushed Jesse closer to ignorance and intolerance and uncertainty so that those two men might just as well have been Ku Klux Klan leaders for all the fear that they evoked in him. And that's how racism so often spreads, not from an act, but from fear of an act.

Jesse joined the North Kirkwood Junior High ninth grade basketball team as a starting forward on our squad. We went 9–0 and set a number of team and individual records. Jesse made his mark with defense and rebounding, setting a tone that would carry into his future years at Kirkwood High. That North team was a monster, starting Bill Tice and me, both at six feet four inches with another athletic, six-foot-four-inch kid, Steve Schaper, coming off the bench. No team came within fifteen points of us as we spent first halves volleyballing rebounds amongst ourselves until we scored, and second halves devoted to second, third, fourth, and fifth stringers running amok.

Our final game that season brought us face to face with a Parkway South team that had won twenty-seven straight games. This was junior high ball, played exclusively before junior high students and players' parents, so Parkway's winning streak was unknown to us and of no particular interest until Coach Sharpe enlightened us the week leading up to the game. One of my Mustang baseball teammates, Tom Burnett, played for Parkway South. His dad, the Mustang coach, Mr. Burnett would be in the stands for the game. That was a motivator for me, not ending some obscure winning streak. The stands were packed that day, the usual one hundred or so students and parents joined by a Parkway South throng occupying every available bleacher seat and standing along the walls at either end of the court. It was the

44

biggest crowd I'd played in front of to date, which generated an intensity I'd not previously encountered.

Parkway South was good. They kept it close with good interior defense and a ball control offense. When they pulled even midway through the third quarter, I realized that it was the first time our starters were even still in the game let alone facing a tie. South had the ball and worked patiently for a short jumper, which they missed. I rebounded, kicked it to Jesse out past the top of the key, and then sprinted up the left side of the court just a few feet from the cheerleaders in front of the crowded bleachers. Jesse hit me with a return pass just past midcourt, and as I put down my first dribble, I saw just one player to beat as he sprinted back on *D*. I dribbled in from the left side, crossed in front of the rim, and then put it up right-handed as the defender could only watch. The crowd noise grew steadily, building to a crescendo, as I realized that my hand and the ball were over the rim as I laid it in to a roar.

It was my first adrenaline cocktail. Start with the game, freeze a pass and a dribble, stir in a defender in pursuit, shake in a tie game situation, and then sprinkle several portions of crowd noise and anticipation. I suddenly realized that I could leverage all of that into a little extra hop, a bit of an edge, if I just used it rather than succumbing to it. I ran back down the right side of the court, low-fiving our bench while glancing over at the crowd, which went ballistic. We had the momentum and the crowd, and we were about to outscore this team 27–13 the rest of the way, capping off an undefeated season and surpassing multiple school records. I was en route to scoring twenty-one

45

points and setting a season scoring record. Our team was about to gain our first-ever mention in the *St. Louis Globe-Democrat* newspaper, convincing the Kirkwood High coaches watching that day to enter our locker room and invite four of us up to play in the remaining sophomore team games. And my sole thought as I ran back down court was, "I could have dunked it." I had never dunked, and at that time, dunking was illegal in games, but that crowd had ignited my sneakers and launched me higher than I had ever soared before.

It was The Game that prohibited dunking, not the game. I demurred out of surprise, not obeisance. If I had known I could get up like that, I would have stuffed it. That's the game: me versus you. Coach Sharpe jumped up to direct our defense as the crowd stood screaming. That dunk would have stopped The Game. It would have drawn a technical foul, erased the basket, and given South free throws. It would have changed The Game, but not the outcome. Jesse and I had just teamed up for a moment of dominance and a dunk would have punctuated that moment, not killed it.

This was just a moment's reflection, mine alone. But Jesse had trailed the play, and as I looked down at the defender, I saw Sugar Bear looking up at me, at my hand, and at the ball. We set up on *D*, I glanced his way, and he nodded. He knew.

Chapter 3

We shake hands. Stolle looks right into my eyes with utter sincerity, like he's extending his hand to help me to my feet or to help a little old lady cross the road. His lips move and I think he's saying, "Good luck," but the din of the old Fieldhouse absorbs his words along with any other sound and all of the oxygen, and any thought of returning his pleasantry is canceled out for lack of air and opportunity. I nod, but he doesn't see as he rubs his hands again and glances down at the center circle.

It was an honest handshake and that's not always the case. At this point, we'd warmed up, but not yet locked horns. As far as the game goes, this is first blood. If we're on the playground or in a gym and it's just the two of us, we're going to shoot for first possession, a rite full of posturing and influence as we each try to gain an edge. "Shoot for outs." If I'm shooting it, I want to show the other guy that I'm not going to miss. If he's shooting it, I'm trying to throw him off. It's less about who gets it out than who wins this first psychological edge.

But this is The Game, so we jump center. I've been jumping center since my sophomore year. I used to be the eager beaver, shaking the other guy's hand and covering it with my off hand, nodding and paying all kinds of homage, so happy just to be there and thrilled to know you, sir, thank you very much. Gradually, I realized that

47

although The Game dictates that we jump center, the jump is really part of the game. Some guys would growl and squeeze it, "I'm stronger than you and I'm gonna squash you the whole game like I'm squashing your hand right now." Others would forgo it altogether, glance down at the hand extended like, "What do you think you're going to do with that?" But John Reed of Webster Groves takes the cake. He'd drift into the circle as though deep in thought, a faraway look in his eyes. Then he'd move his hand just off his hip so you'd reach for it, damn near falling over to grab it, and when you did, you were left holding a stone-cold, lifeless, emotionless, and completely repulsive dead fish, while John stared just past your face, no doubt reveling in your discomfort behind his dreadful mask.

The ref tosses it up and I can see it's a foot off center, directly over Stolle's head, and I slap at it, but he's tipped it back to his guy. Bad toss, but Stolle was up. I'm not sure I'd have won it anyway. They walk it up, reverse it once, and 22 lets fly an eighteen footer. So much for them stalling. That took about ten seconds. It misses and so do the next couple of shots for both teams. We're tight, they're tight, and I can't draw a full breath, plus that noise is in my head, so I can't even hear my guys call out the defensive switches.

Raytown gets a cheapie off an inbounds play to lead 2–0 and Tommy gets one back on a free throw after he's already missed a couple short. That make is our first chance to press, and I realize it's gone quiet, not the Fieldhouse, because it's still noisy as hell in here, but my head is as still as glass. I remember sitting on the bottom of the shallow end of the pool wearing my swim mask looking up through the water at people up on the deck, and it feels just like that now. I'm submerged in this giant pool and I'm looking out at the fans and can't hear anything.

48

It's just like looking through that swim mask, except everything's not yellow. I can't even hear Mr. Miller's voice as he shouts out a press, but I know what to run anyway because when we're pressing, we're in a comfort zone, the press as familiar and calming as one's favorite pair of shoes. It's still surreal in here, but defensively we're starting to find a rhythm, starting to contest passes and deny cutters, and I try to draw a deep breath. I try to find that second wind and it's not there yet, but it will be soon. Just let the game come to you, that's what everyone says, and now we're a couple of minutes in and The Game is out there, up in the stands, but the game is right here. The game has come to me and it's coming to my guys, and we're fine. I can handle 52 and cheat to Stolle if I need to, but Rock's denying him the ball, and I don't see anyone else out here who's going to hurt us.

Except Raytown's not feeling that way. They're going about their business like little robots, squaring up, two-hand chest passing to cutters running precise routes, oblivious to our pressure, whether through ignorance or indifference, I can't tell. We continue to press and we go man and Tommy's all over 30 as he dribbles into the frontcourt, it comes loose and Billy just misses the steal, so they swing it hurriedly to 22 for a pull up nineteen footer, and Tommy is in his grill so the guy misses badly. We disrupt every pass, every dribble, and finally, the shot. It's an ugly possession for them, but they don't seem to notice—no shouts, no dropping their heads, no panic. And as the shot goes up, both guards are already retreating, so they don't contest the rebound, which Rock grabs with ease. It's like it's all part of a plan, some bigger picture they have for this situation, for this entire game.

Another minute passes and 52 misses a free throw. I go up and get the rebound, and Stolle doesn't contest. He was right next to me in the lane, but as I come down with the ball, he's gone, running back down court, so when I outlet it to Tommy, all five of their guys are back on D. There's no chance to run on them. Instead, Tommy pulls up at the free throw line and all five are jammed up in the lane. Billy enters it to me as I flash from the low block into the lane, and it's my first offensive touch, which I fumble. Stolle's late to close, but 22 doubles down, and I can't really get it out of my holster now, so I airball it. I miss so badly that it falls right into Rock's hands and he misses from point blank range. They call a foul, but I put my hands on my hips and stare at him, thinking, "How many times have you made that shot without ever missing until now?" Rock walks to the line and glances back at me like, "How many times has Drew shot that shot without ever once airballing it?" One miss and one make on the free throws, and it's tied 2–2.

So we press, and again, they stumble into the frontcourt like Mr. Magoo wandering across the freeway oblivious as cars race by nearly hitting him. Number 52 puts down a dribble, and from behind, Tommy's got the steal…but no, he fouls him. Number 52 drains the free throw and I notice he's got a real nice stroke from there, so we don't want to keep sending him to the line. Again, they're back, and again, we're moving like we're in quicksand as Rock bricks one from the top of the key. We have no penetration, no edge. What was that about not shooting unless we make them? Well what do we do now since we're not making anything? Again, 52 goes to the line and drains it. I'm looking around at Raytown and it's like the time my family went to a wax museum and all those figures looked just like colonials in their wigs and stockings, but when we got up real close, we could see their sightless eyes and lifeless skin. These guys are so unimpressive up

50

close. They're small and slow and overmatched, but even though I
know it and I think my guys know it, Raytown doesn't know it. They
just keep walking it up and making their cuts, and it's all so predictable
and so ineffective, but still we're down and stuck in some sort of spell
cast by these wax figures. I glance at their bench and half expect to see
voodoo dolls of our starting five bound and gagged, stuck with a
million pins.

Showtime

> Step right up, hurry, hurry
> Before the show begins
> My friends
> Stand in line
> Get your tickets
> I hope you will attend
> —"Sideshow," The Stylistics

"Are you scared?" It was the fall of my eighth-grade year, 1967. My father was driving me to my Junior Cardinals football game at Kirkwood Park, where we were facing an all-black Mathew Dickey team from downtown St. Louis. His words hung in the air between us.

"Scared of what?" The race riots that spread across the country in the early sixties had flashed by me, but it was only a glimpse, a couple of newsreel clips I caught as I settled down in front of the TV for *F Troop* or *Gilligan's Island*. They were real as in real far away. The black power movement was marching

51

forward and onto the front page, but to a thirteen-year-old kid, it was noise. I was on my way to a game. That was all.

"Well, sometimes, uh…." He wasn't expecting to have to explain it to me. "Sometimes blacks or black teams can…intimidate you…if you're white." It was dark in the car and I think we were both glad to not be able to see each other's embarrassment, he for having said it and me for having to hear him.

"Coach warned us they might play dirty." But that wasn't because they were black; it was because he had scouted them and he'd seen a couple of incidents. "He said if that happens to just tell the ref and keep on playing." Dad said nothing. "We put in two new pass plays," I continued. "I'm going to score at least one touchdown."

We crouched for the first play from scrimmage and their linebacker got down in front of Mark Lind, right in his face. "Boy, I'm gonna break your f'ing arm," he bellowed. "Come ahead on," growled Lind, proceeding to blow that linebacker onto his back and then he piled on top of him as Mark Harter ripped off a ten-yard gain right through that hole. We went on to win 33–6 and I scored two touchdowns on passes from Pat Morley. We respected that team and we feared them because they'd been winning their games and they were bullies, but not because they were black. As far as the game went, it was just them and us in the trenches—come ahead on. Both teams were just young teenage boys playing a game. It was up in the stands and back in our car where prejudice and bias resided.

The black power movement was confusing. In one corner stood the moderate influence of the NAACP and Martin Luther King. In another was the Black Panther Party, a more aggressive movement led by Bobby Seale and Huey Newton. In between stood the opportunists, blacks and whites who were just looking for an excuse to fight. Segregation or integration? Politics or violence? And closer to home—my home and even the homes of those Matthew Dickey players—was the game. Line up and play, face the guy across from you and try to beat him, knock him on his butt or run by him to haul down a pass. Maybe he trounces on you after the whistle and the ref chooses to ignore it because if he throws a flag on that black team, it's going to cause a stir. Just a few more flags later, it's the fans and the coaches feeding the fire, and since that black player was just trying for an edge or perhaps even acting out his frustration because his guys are in the process of getting blown out, since that kid was just trying to win the game rather than support a civil rights movement, and his impulse to behave that way in the game was probably instilled in him by those same external forces and not this competition, within that entire context, let's not validate the act or assign any greater significance to it than the lame attempt at bullying that it was. And most of all, let's not violate the game this time, and instead let the kids play it out rather than the adults duke it out, and maybe, ultimately, it's an investment in the game and these kids.

Less than two months prior to that youth football game, in a gesture reviewed and reviled by millions, black athletes John Carlos and Tommy Smith raised black-gloved fists at the

1968 Olympic Games in Mexico City. A few days later at that same Olympics, nineteen-year-old George Foreman raised a tiny American flag held in his boxing glove immediately after winning the heavyweight gold medal. Carlos and Smith were hard-working student athletes and future coaches and leaders. Foreman was a dropout and a street thug. But based on each simple act, Foreman became an icon in the eyes of the American public, while Smith and Carlos were suspended by the US team and banned from the Olympic Village.

I rooted hard for all three of them, at least within the game. As sporting events went, this was transcendent. It was the United States against the Soviet Union, Democracy versus Communism, good versus evil. Smith and Carlos were maintaining America's dominance in the sprints when they ran first and third in the two hundred meter finals, and Foreman destroyed Russian Ionas Chepulis in the gold medal match, all of which we watched on TV, screaming at the top of our lungs, not because we knew or had anything in common with the three of them, but in support of our guys versus the other guys in a game.

I watched Muhammad Ali's fights on our tiny, black-and-white set in the basement some time before Dad's home improvement project and our subsequent destruction of his panels and tiling. I'd dance around the concrete floor shadowboxing between rounds and Ali became my favorite athlete by far. He was banned from boxing for three years beginning in 1967 for taking a stand against the Vietnam War and refusing induction after he'd been drafted. If that had been a white athlete like Mickey Mantle or Joe Namath, the reaction would have been limited to their decision, but in Ali's case, it quickly expanded to race and, given Ali's conversion to Islam, religion. His quote, "I ain't got no quarrel with them Viet Congs," would resonate with me five years later when I was facing the specter of the draft. To me, it was a fair argument then and going forward. So while some people hated him for his association with Malcolm X and Islam, and others hated him for refusing the draft, I admired his athleticism and skill. He was fun to watch.

Out of this confusion rose Tommy Grice, who always seemed to have a lot on his mind, like a scientist wrestling with a knotty problem or a doctor pondering an incurable disease. The day that several of us North Junior High players attended a hoop game at our sister junior high, Nipher, I got a chance to see Tommy for the first time. And he did not disappoint. We walked into the gym just after the opening tip to see the Nipher cheerleaders, mostly black, dancing and singing to Marvin Gaye. "I heard it through the grapevine Nipher's gonna beat Mehlville, baby." The stands were full and in the top row sat a couple of Kirkwood High coaches surveying the other half of their incoming freshmen players.

A black Nipher player blew by his defender and took the ball straight at the rim, scoring over a second defender, and I knew who I was seeing without a program. Moments later, Mehlville was shooting free throws and I saw Tommy glance our way. That's all it was, just a quick look, and then hands on hips and eyes on the ground. But that brief spark was all it took to light the fuse for Showtime and twenty-five points later, Tommy had made his point and the game was a blowout. As he came out of the game, Showtime high-fived a couple of his teammates and walked to the end of the bench for some water, standing there, cup in hand, and he stared across the floor over to our bleachers. His gaze was fixed, not on the high school coaches or on us. He was staring at his classmates in the bleachers, some black and some white, and they stood as one and gave him an ovation. He remained stoic, taking a pull on his water and dropping the cup, and then taking a seat. He had talent, desire, and focus. He possessed a deep-seated fire that burned inside pushing him to excel and to win, and he was connected to his class as though he carried them with him to whatever heights he could achieve.

My first thought was a selfish one: we could beat Nipher even though we wouldn't be playing them. Tommy was good and so was Sam Weaver, their big man, but we could handle them. My second thought was Tommy, the way he handled the ball, his speed and toughness and his shot. He was going to be a hell of a teammate. I also realized right then that Tommy Grice was capable of scoring a lot of points at Kirkwood High. A few weeks later, immediately following our final junior high game, several of us drew a visit from the high school B team coach, Paul Meyer. One minute we were whooping it up in the shower, reveling in the several weeks of freedom that awaited before baseball practice would begin, and the next minute we were pondering tomorrow's B team practice and wondering how short-lived our newfound hiatus had become.

A couple players from Nipher had been invited up to the B team as well. I entered the B team locker room that first day and found Tommy alone, hunched over his sneakers and lacing them up tight. He was compact and tightly knit and so absorbed in thought that he didn't see me standing there. He got his sneakers laced up and leaned forward, gripping the bench with both hands, and then stared at the lockers before him so long and so intently that I thought maybe he was looking for a towel or a shirt inside.

I had a lot on my mind at that point, like why in the world had this been the day that Mrs. Parham caught me chewing gum as I left school and why had she felt compelled to take me to the principal's office and write me a yellow slip. The ordeal took forty-five minutes to boot, so even after running the half-mile to the high school, I was now late for my first B team practice. And I had the distinct impression that Tommy's thoughts ran much deeper, although given the yellow slip that was burning a hole in my pocket, it was impossible for me to fathom exactly what that might be. I would soon learn the exact nature and subject of his preoccupation, but at that moment I needed to hurry up.

Tommy glanced up at me and our eyes met, and I knew who he was and he knew who I was, and so nothing needed to be said. But something was going to be said because I was never good about silence. That's the only reason we spoke as it became abundantly clear that Tommy was a man of very few words and might just as well have headed out to practice without a word and proceeded to maintain that silence forever, not because he was antagonistic or shy, but because he had nothing to say and wasn't much for idle chatter. Plus, we weren't yet teammates. We were about to become teammates, but at that moment, having just commuted from our respective junior highs and having each considered our respective prospects had our teams met, no doubt sharing a confidence that each would have beaten the other, with all that hanging in the air and about to join a dozen sophomores who probably resented our intrusion, we both paused.

"Hey, Tommy," I said.

"You're late." He offered me his hand and we shook. He stood to go, closing his locker behind him.

"Well, save me some, okay?"

"Uh huh."

He stepped past me and walked to the door, his stride smooth and efficient like a jaguar ready to pounce. Showtime, that was his nickname, but he didn't show anything. Tommy had transferred to Nipher from archrival Webster Groves just a year earlier. He'd parlayed his incredible athletic talent into football, basketball, and track prowess, which had gained him notoriety and friendships. During that ninth grade year, Tommy wrestled his way to the intramural championships, where he faced Gary Wallace, a white kid just as athletic and just as popular. Both Tommy and Gary were friends with tons of blacks and whites; they were probably as non-racially biased as any two kids at Nipher. They were teammates in football and friends. But when they took to the mat that afternoon, the gym was packed and divided, whites over here and blacks over there.

The two of them bore the burden of those two sides, like it or not. This was not a racial encounter, not a venue for blacks to fight whites, but it was a contest between representatives of their two races, and in the absence of raw animosity stood pride and competition and credibility. Neither race sought supremacy or violence, but every kid in that gym was rooting hard for his guy, for affirmation that their guy was better than the other guy. Tommy lost that match and so took responsibility, graciously accepting the outcome while seething inside, not so much for what it did to the other black kids, but for what it had done to him. Tommy was harder on himself than any parent or teacher or coach could ever be.

Tommy Grice was the one member of our high school hoop team in who the game and The Game coexisted. He played both together simultaneously, taking on his opponent while carrying the hopes and expectations of his friends and even his race into each venue and across each hardwood floor. As such, he saw each situation that arose deeper and pondered harder than any of the rest of us. Tommy wanted to win and he savored the competition, but always with a furrowed brow and tight lips. I imagined him at home before and after every game, staring at his two hands, one encased in a black leather glove and the other gripping a tiny American flag.

North and Nipher's combined record that year was 18–3. Up at the high school the sophomores were enduring the worst B team record in school history, so it was no surprise that most of us freshmen were given significant roles when we arrived. Tommy and I became starters. Three nights later, we played our first game, at University City on a Friday night. This was one of only two teams the B team had beaten, so expectations were high and so was the pressure. By supplanting two sophomore starters, the team ought to play better and certainly must get a win, or what did that say about us?

B team games were among the best kept secrets in the world back then. Scheduled two hours before the varsity games and during rush hour to boot, I'd never seen one. Judging by the dearth of spectators at the opening tip, neither had anyone else. The game was faster and more physical than freshman ball, and Tommy and I made the adjustment as the game wore on, but it remained close throughout. And just like in a storybook, there I stood at the free throw line with ten seconds remaining to shoot one-and-one trailing by a point. U City called a time-out, just to be sure I grasped the gravity of the situation, and had some time to assimilate.

I'd begun to learn the difference between the game and The Game, so I wasn't all that nervous about the shots. Same thing as in the neighbor's driveway, easier in fact because there was no snow or puddle and no wind. Piece of cake. Plus, there were ten seconds remaining, an eternity compared to the two seconds when I'd play the Russians. The Game was no issue at all. However, as I stepped to the line, my mind became crowded with random thoughts. I was fifteen years old.

I lacked a free throw routine. Most guys develop something automatic, like bounce, bounce, bounce, hold the ball, spin it, look at the rim, bend, and extend. But not me. Instead, I looked around and spotted the varsity team, peering out the locker room door, impatiently tapping their feet because our game had run long and they didn't want overtime to delay it further. "Miss," a couple of them mimed. There was no help there. Next, I looked to Coach Meyer hoping for some encouragement, but as I looked at him, I remembered the ninth grade party set for that night, and the contrivance that Bill Tice and I had cooked up to gain Meyer's permission to leave right after our game rather than wait for the varsity game, and how the subsequent bus ride home wouldn't land us at KHS before ten or half past. We needed an excuse to join our friends who were getting picked up right after our game to catch a ride to the party. But at that moment, I needed to focus on my free throws. I took the ball from the official, and as I did, I peered over his shoulder and happened to notice that the gym was filling with the varsity game now just minutes away, unless I happened to make one and miss one and send that measly B team game into OT, which the varsity teams didn't want and several hundred fans didn't want either. I imagined they were all miming "Miss!" A quick check of the upper deck bleachers produced the image of those friends—the ones who would give us a ride—backed up against a wall by several U City toughs about to fork over their lunch money under extreme duress. They'd be out of there as soon as that transaction ended, unless watches and wallets were extracted. Regardless, they'd be sprinting for their dad's family wagon and wouldn't likely wait around for us, so whatever excuse we cooked up for Coach Meyer had to include alternative transportation, presuming we emerged intact and with our own lunch money. Oh, and about those free throws...I bounced it

61

once and gazed up at the rim, settling back into the game and the comfort of the neighbor's driveway, no ice, no wind, but it was a glass blackboard and transparent, and those empty upper-deck bleachers that so nicely framed my earlier free throws were at once crawling with U City fans gesturing and contorting and leering at me right through the backboard. I was seeing the hallucinogenic scenes from Disney's *Fantasia* through my very own backboard only without the music.

My free throw barely moved the net as it dropped through. Only it didn't drop through. It barely touched the net as I short-armed it two feet short. U City rebounded, Kirkwood fouled, their guy drained both free throws because those were his friends beaming through the glass backboard. Game over. Furious sophomores pushed past us into the locker room, barking about the freshmen who'd screwed up their last chance to win a game. Tommy looked at me like, "That's it?" Coach Meyer consoled me, explaining that when guys get nervous, they always shoot short, and how it was his fault for not warning me while I thought, "Well, it is kind of your fault, but not for the reason you think."

Tice sat next to me in the locker room while everyone else maintained leper distance. We began to plot our escape. If that party had contributed to my distraction, then we sure as hell would be attending. With two young, creative minds on the planning, Tice felt pretty sure he could call his dad to pick us up, which meant we just needed an excuse to split. This is what we came up with: "We're leaving tonight to go hunting." Yep. Forget the fact that I had never been hunting in my life and Tice

62

probably hadn't either, and forget the fact that we didn't have any info to survive a follow-up question should Coach Meyer ask one, and forget that there were far simpler, more credible excuses that had been available to us. That's the story we concocted. And here's how the conversation went:

Us: "Coach Meyer, we have to leave early and can't ride home on the bus."

Him: "Why?"

Us: "We're leaving tonight to go hunting."

Him: "What are you going to hunt?"

We responded in unison.

Tice: "Bear."

Me: "Deer."

Our jumbled response sounded like *beer*, so over the next two hours, which we spent sitting though the varsity game, and through the hour after that, spent waiting for the team to shower and then taking the bus back home, we had plenty of time to assess just how Coach Meyer might have seen through our clever ruse. We sorted through all possibilities: he thought we said *beer* and we were underage, plus no one really hunts beer; he brilliantly deduced that we were hunting different animals as neither deer nor bear were in season; there is no bear hunting in or around St. Louis County because there are no bears. Not once did we consider the fact that we were young and stupid and Coach was well aware, not even as we ran extra laps after Monday's practice. Instead, we figured that if we'd both said *rabbit* we would have made that party.

Tuesday was another game and a much-appreciated chance to wipe away the U City experience. Tommy played well. In fact, all of the freshmen played well. I had nineteen points and adjusted to the physical play, blocking out for rebounds, and pushing around and over defenders to score. It was a home game, my first on the KHS floor, and the old metal backboards were a comfort and a relief. The next day after school, I sprinted out the door for practice only to be halted and chastened by Mrs. Parham again, this time for failing to hold the door open for her. Although I escaped a yellow slip, I was subjected to a finger-pointing lecture about manners and decorum and respect, none of which I really heard, but all of which I was convinced was intended to deflate her perception of an egotistical jock leveraging his elevation to the high school team into free reign at the junior high. It all seemed so false and unfair; nonetheless, she'd demonstrated to us both her power and station, and my subservience to both.

So for the second time in a week, I sprinted into the high school locker room, sweaty and late, so late that the room was empty and silent except for the muffled pounding of balls on the court through the old cement walls. I plopped down on a bench and began frantically changing into my gym clothes when from behind me I heard, "Rogers, you score nineteen points one night and you think you can come and go as you please. Is that it?" I glanced up at Mr. Miller and thought I saw just a trace of a smile, but it might have been wishful thinking. For that matter, it might have been a scowl. Mr. Miller sat down on a bench opposite me and told me to stop what I was doing and listen.

Chapter 4

I'd never thought about how short an eight-minute quarter is. When we're pressing and breaking, we're getting twenty or more shots a quarter and scoring twenty plus points. But when a team deflates the ball and slows things to a crawl like these guys are doing, there aren't many shots. And when nothing's going in, we're stuck in park. With half a quarter gone, we have no field goals—none. Zero, zip, nada, blotto. My only touch was that airball, and all our shots have been jumpers except for Rock's point blank miss. As games go, this one's no fun. There've been no matchups, no challenges, no sequences in which I've faced my guy, and he's come right back and stuck it to me. It's a sleepwalk. At 4–2, we've each got just two free throws plus one stinking field goal between us. What the hell!?

This has nothing to do with a state final and thousands of fans; that whole deal is long gone and worlds away. This is about a succession of dull possessions and boring hoop, walking up and down the floor then back and forth to the free throw line. Billy tries his luck and misses, so now it's officially an epidemic. Nobody can make a shot, which means we can't press, which denies us our run outs, and plays right into their hands, their sallow, little hands like sculptors' hands, twisting and shaping us, pulling and pressing us, making us into exactly their shapes and squeezing out any semblance of who we were when we took the floor carrying that thirty-one game winning streak

65

and buoyed by the devastation we'd always inflicted. The Pattonville coach said we beat his guys so badly at Christmas that they never recovered. That's who we are — or were, before this bunch got ahold of us. Rock fouls and Tommy misses a jump shot and although each one of us is as cold as ice, Tommy is Frosty the Snowman. I glance over at the Raytown coach, who's a lot younger than Mr. Miller and waving his hands around not frantically but slowly and purposefully, wide sweeps like he's conducting a symphony. No, it's like he's a puppeteer. He is Geppetto and we are his puppets. He's just pulling the strings courtside and we're helpless to resist.

Raytown's ice cold, too. I rebound a miss and see Tommy streaking long. I'm cocked to fire it out, but Billy's right there demanding it, so I hand it to him and take off. Billy pushes it ahead to Tommy and we're early enough that Raytown's not set. When I break to the elbow, Stolle's late, so not only is there space, he's rushing to catch up, then bingo — there it is. I don't think, I don't react. My brain has abdicated and my body takes over. It's just instinct, very basic. If you catch and you're balanced and the other guy is moving one way, you just move the other way. There's no rush because he's still got to land and change direction. When players speak of things slowing down in games like this, they're mistaken or else they're misinterpreting. The game hasn't slowed down. They've sped up. They've eliminated the time wasted when the brain says to do something before doing it. Now they're just doing without any intrusion from the brain to describe how to do it. The body just knows.

As I gather it in, the leather ball feels smooth and firm, so easy to grip. I hold it for just an instant, but it feels as familiar as a favorite stuffed animal, worn and contoured, fitting my person and comforting

66

me. I've not thought ahead, haven't decided what to do when I catch the ball because I've caught it hundreds of times before with my back to the basket along the right side of the key, just below the free throw line. Just create space and shoot with no need to form the thought— just do it.

There are probably four or five moves I might make from here, and my body chooses the oldest and the surest. Stolle's moving toward the free throw line behind me, so I drop my left shoulder, make one power dribble toward the baseline, and take a kick step. It's no ordinary kick step, but a genuine, marching drum major, Rockettes chorus line, black belt karate man, foot at hip level, space-eating kick step that takes me from back there to the baseline while Stolle's landing and recovering, but he's gonna be late and short and he leaps to contest this bad boy and sure enough, it's gone and he's flying in front of me, and I can just peak over that wretched haircut of his to see the net splash, and I feel that tug on the fishing line felt when I'm in a zone and that ball is just a dart I'm flicking at the bull's-eye.

And just like that, the game's tied 4–4. With the make, they take it out, we're pressing, and now it's a game again. I can feel Stolle eyeing me and I won't give him the satisfaction of returning his gaze, because my guns are oiled and ready and just itching to shoot again. My hand's on my holster and my fingers twitch and I take a quick look at Geppetto. The only reason I don't feign shooting him right between the eyes is because I'm saving all my bullets for the basket. I'm gonna shoot up his whole posse, and when all those toy cowboys are strewn across the floor, steaming and spent, I'll have saved one last bullet for him.

It was that kick step that got me in my rhythm, an unconventional move I picked up years ago. Cecil Jones used to do it and I liked the way it looked, that's all. Nobody approached me to teach me or explain its use. I just liked how Cecil looked when he did it and I wanted to look that same way. Thousands of tries later, my body bypassed my brain and pulled it out, using it to score Kirkwood's first field goal in the state championship game, a million miles and countless eons from its humble origins at the Kirkwood Community Center.

Kirkwood's 1ˢᵗ hoop vs. Raytown.
I'm shooting and Stolle's defending.

The Center

People let me tell you about a place I know
To get in it don't take much dough
Where you can really do your thing, oh yeah
...People gather there from all parts of town
        —"Psychedelic Shack," The Temptations

That's where I learned to play. Built in 1966, the Center was located in South Kirkwood, close enough to Meacham Park to be easily accessible by blacks and still far enough north to feel safe for whites. The Center provided a common area for both groups, though it was well short of any kind of melting pot. The atmosphere inside was 100 percent soul; the mix of hoop players ran 90 percent black. The first time I ventured inside, I was one of two white players total. I cowered just inside the main door, straining to adjust my eyes from the brilliant sunlight to the grainy shadows cast by the fading, fluorescent light fixtures, several of which were burned out. They looked like bats flapping in a cave. I remembered Oscar Robertson saying that he learned to shoot at night where he could barely make out the front of the orange rim. I figured the light in the Center was just as bad.

The court appeared cramped and worn, the sidelines extending to within five feet of three of the side walls, with a seven- or eight-foot space from the remaining wall. That gap served as a dumping ground for coats and gear, and it was

69

populated by younger black kids, throwing jacks or playing with dolls, safe and warm away from the elements. At first glance, it looked like a small piece of Meacham Park, ripped away and dropped down at Kirkwood Park. It was a microcosm of soul and jive, rife with characters and caricatures. From blaxploitation gangsters sporting huge Afros and heavy boots to lean, hungry athletes, to girls and boys performing impromptu cartwheels, racing and soaring up and down the basketball floor.

Cecil Jones told me about the Center. He was a starting junior guard at KHS my freshman year, and when our group showed up for B team practice, he'd watch us trudge out to the court. He'd chatter, speaking mostly nonsense and harmless quips, and he began to call me Young Boy. Cecil was both intimidating and captivating. Then one day, as he walked through our practice, he caught me missing a shot in traffic. "Young Boy!" he called out. "Make some space for that shot."

Toweling off in the locker room later, Cecil called over his shoulder, "Next year, Young Boy, you gonna be up here." He yanked up his trousers and turned to face me, his round eyes big and earnest. "So you got to get busy." I nodded. "What?" he asked, imitating my nod. "What does that mean?" His smile was a prank, like he'd just put a lit match under my toes, waiting for me to burn. "Why you nodding? Do you know what I'm saying?" I mumbled something. "Get your ass to the Center and get yourself some game, Young Boy. Get you something more than that driveway shit you playing right now."

So there it was. On a cold, spring, Saturday morning a few days later, I stood among the coats and jump ropes along that near wall, shifting from one foot to the other, clinging to my sneakers and trying to make out the players amidst the dim shadows and the cacophony of indecipherable trash talking. "You got this? Bet! You ain't got shit.! Money!" Finally I saw Cecil kick- stepping to the middle and pulling up to shoot. I caught his eye, and at that point, in this place he didn't know me, didn't see me, didn't give a rat's ass about me.

My anonymity afforded some time and space to check out the game once my eyes had finally adjusted. It looked pretty standard: half-court three-on-three, with players of all shapes and sizes from teenage to early thirties, plus nonstop trash talking and arguing.

"Foul!"

"Foul? Bullshit!"

Silence. The player would stand, hand on hip, his other hand outstretched insisting on the ball.

"What? This ain't yours. I didn't touch you."

Silence, hand outstretched, perturbed look.

"Man, you crazy. Just because you missed don't mean…"

"Shoot for it."

"Man, we ain't shootin' for it when all he did was miss."

"The man made a call. You may not like it, but you got to respect it."

"I ain't respectin' shit. He don't get any respect beggin' like that."

"Shoot it! Damn, nigger, it's only 1–1. You can't be stopping every play 'til game."

71

But they did stop and they did argue every play, every call, and every shot. As I watched, a pecking order emerged. The oldest players carried the most sway and spoke the least. When one of the older players shot and missed, no call was made. Instead, the shooter would stop in the middle of play, hold out his hand, and stare at the floor, shaking his head disgustedly. No one could play on because he stood in the way. What's more, no one could argue since the protest was nonverbal. That left it to the next tier of players—the best and boldest—to respectfully question the nonexistent call.

"Brother, what you saying? Who? Who got you? Me? Damn! I didn't get you. That was all ball!"

Pause. Then silence as the player would calmly take the ball from another guy's hand while the protestor continued. "Well it ain't yours, then. We're at least gonna shoot for it."

The player would spin the ball in his hands at the top of the key and hand it to the protestor who announced. "Okay, then. I'm gonna shoot for it."

The player would shake his head and extend his hand to get the ball back; no arguing his call. The protestor was forced to oblige, griping for the ensuing five minutes about the call.

Somewhere deep down, way at the bottom of that hierarchy, is where I took up residence; I fell just above pariah, but well below new and stupid. The clout required to enforce a silent call arose through age, proficiency, and a whole lot of time at the Center, so much time that few players remembered anything about your pre-Center career and whether you were ever any good, thus empowering you to claim credibility based

72

on rumor and lore, testimony to the saying, "the longer it's been, the better I used to be."

Cecil lacked that tenure, but he had plenty of game. He was long and smooth, a tall guard with a great handle and a pretty good jumper. He was part of Kirkwood High's state championship cross country team and so he possessed endless stamina, which came in handy during extended games and arguments.

Games went to eleven straight. Winners kept the court, while losers rushed to determine who had next, begging their way into the next game. When it was crowded, a loss could mean waiting up to an hour to play again, so players stacked their teams and fought like mad to win. Professional golfer Lee Trevino used to snicker at those who asked if he felt pressure standing over a big putt in a PGA match. "You don't know what pressure is until you've played for $5 with only $2 in your pocket." he said. Pressure at the Center felt similar. Forget crowds or leagues. I didn't want to lose because the right to play on was precious. And I sure as hell didn't want to miss the shot or give up the shot that led to my team's loss. That would destroy my right to play on, the penalty being isolation, resentment, and ultimately, banishment. There's no way I'd be able to even beg my way onto another team no matter how long I waited. Games would end, everyone would leave, and there I'd stand, wearing my shame in solitude, hoping a week would suffice to erase things and let me start anew.

So from a score of about seven on, everyone ceased driving to the hoop because doing so brought a foul on every play. Always. The only penalty for fouling was ball out to the offensive team. There were no free throws and no cumulative foul counts, so no one could foul out. The defense was free to foul to prevent every easy shot. This created a premium on creating space rather than gaining a step; jump shots outweighed taking it to the rim. It was a game of individual moves, outside shots, and no free throws, factors which ultimately shaped our high school team and defined our strengths and weaknesses right up to the night we played Raytown South.

Cecil's game ended when an opposing player drained a long one. Even before it splashed the net, the losers were already poring over the small crowd along the near wall.

"Who's got next? You?"

"Who's got next? You? Well who you got? Man, you don't want him! Pick me up. Yeah! Hell, he can wait one more. Ain't no big thing. You want to win, don't you? Now who else we got?"

Twenty minutes later, the crowd had thinned. I was on a first-name basis with every small kid along the near wall. I'd held the rope and counted cadence for nearly all of the small jump-roping kids. As another game ended, I glanced up, hopeful, and noticed that only a few players were still waiting. Cecil had next. He grabbed two of the three losers coming off the court. Both ignored him and headed for the door. With his hands on his hips, Cecil gazed down the near wall. There was a black kid with horn-rimmed glasses wearing dress shorts and a button-down shirt and me. Cecil looked past us at the girls jumping rope. "No, please," I thought. "Not them."

"James," Cecil said to Horn-Rims. "Go get Harvey." Horn-Rims scooted past me and out the door. "I got Harvey," Cecil said over his shoulder, eyeing me. "Young Boy." I paused. That's it. Am I in? "See if there's anyone else outside who can play." Damn! Then Cecil's eyes got big and round. "Man, don't look like that. I'm just playin'. C'mon, let's go."

I hadn't shot in half an hour as other players came and went, so I was ice cold. I grabbed the game ball and launched a twenty-foot warm-up shot that sailed over the hoop. "Damn, Young Boy."

"We got it out," said Ricky Nelson, asking for the ball. After my long sentence on the sideline, I'd learned that he had deformed, curled-up toes from when he was young as his folks couldn't afford large enough shoes. Nelson had some game and a little of that old guy cred. Cecil grabbed the ball and shook his head. I glanced at Ricky's shoes, which seemed pretty small for a guy his size. I wondered if the toe story was for real.

"Man, it's ours," insisted Ricky. "Look at your team. You got Harvey and now you got six-seven dude!" That was me. I was six-foot-four and skinny, less imposing than Horn-Rims who'd just run out the door in his preppy shirt and shorts never to return. But Ricky's cred outranked Cecil's prowess. Cecil tossed the ball to Ricky and then glanced at me. "Don't you dare shoot, Young Boy. Either pick for me or get out of the way, but don't shoot it." And I didn't, not that game at least. But I went back up to the Center the next week and the one after that, working my way up the caste system, soon achieving an improved rank: "If you get a rebound, you can shoot that one, but you sure as hell better make it or don't think about shooting another one even if it is a rebound." It was a grudging progress marked by pale shades of credibility.

Over the years, I shaped my skills at the Center, watching the best ball handlers and learning to protect the ball as I made my way through the hornet's nest of slaps and grabs, keeping my balance against the shoves and shoulders, developing a quick pull up and release to create that vital space and squeeze off my shot before the leapers could get to it. And most of all, I sprouted armor, the physical strength to absorb contact and the emotional fortitude to make a move, make a call, and make it stand up. I also fostered a number of relationships there, friendships based on mutual respect because in that gym, we were joined in an effort to maintain almighty court ownership, locked in the struggle to wrest it or protect it from the others. In these battles, one's sense of self evacuated leaving only the player engaged in the game, the outcome of which defined one's very life on that court. One might succeed and play on to the next game or fail and be sentenced to purgatory, the interminable wait for redemption or the arduous trudge to the door, to the cold, and into the snow beyond.

So, you worked with those other guys, sliding to pick up their man when they got beat, doubling down on that post-up opponent, picking for your shooter, and rolling to an open spot in case they switched, shoving for rebound position like the last guy into the elevator before the door closes. And when that game got to nine- all or ten- all, you grabbed at your share of the rope and pulled with your teammates as one with no regard for their curled-up toes or trash-talking mouths. All that mattered by then, after twenty-plus minutes of playing and posturing, arguing and leveraging, when every guy's arsenal was discharged, and legs were exhausted, and sweat was pouring off, and you realized that an hour or two later when you're in that hot shower scrubbing the scratches and bruises and squeezing life back into your limbs, and for the rest of the day and maybe even the next day, your state of mind would be defined by the outcome of the game—of *this* game. The Center bonded us as a foxhole does soldiers.

But such alliances existed only within those four walls, only within the game. On the street or away from the Center, all external rules applied: race, money, neighborhood, employment, school—none of which existed in the Center, but all of which were divisive, dictating life on the outside. As it turned out, Ricky Nelson attended Kirkwood High during my sophomore year. Still, despite a number of Center games, we never spoke at school. Harvey Love was a year older than I and one of the warmest and funniest blacks I knew. A terrific athlete, Love was only a marginal hoop player. More than once, we collaborated to produce Center victories. I made baskets and he offered physical defense and a stout representation in arguments and occasional fights. We were football teammates for two years and he pounded me with a vengeance in practice. We were also baseball teammates and used to clown around on the bench. Harvey would predict, "I'm gonna spike that first baseman if I ground out." Sure enough, he'd flash across the bag and that first baseman would wince and grab his ankle. We'd all laugh as Harvey kept running up the right field line with his mouth open, howling. But in the hallways, Love and I were strangers.

In those days, there was no admission charge to join or enter the Center, and there was no security. Anyone could wander in off the street and nearly everyone did. The cast of characters back then was broad, diverse, and as unpredictable as a tornado; it was also nearly as volatile. Larry Philips was a KHS grad, five or six years older than I, who had reached the top level of credibility, which he carried with quiet confidence. Philips was big and strong, with a sizable rear he used to back you down. He had great balance and footwork with which he could spin away and launch short jumpers with a touch as soft as a nanny's. People called him Loose Booty, the origin of which was tied to the girls he chased, though its perpetuity was a product of his own backside. No one ever called him Larry, and no one ever shortened the nickname. Even during arguments, it was, "Loose Booty, there's no way I fouled you!" Or, "C'mon, Loose Booty, give it up!" In games, guys shouted, "Switch! I got Loose Booty and you got mine!" And for all the effort required to continually use his full nickname, Loose Booty himself was a man of few words. He'd look off into the distance and speak in a soft, but distinct voice. "I got next," he'd say, and although one may not have heard his exact words, we could figure it out and respected it nonetheless. A few years later, the summer after I had transferred from Kansas University to the local junior college, I wandered into the gym one night where Loose Booty was playing pickup. As I walked past, he backed his man down for the inevitable spin away and shoot. "Rog-iss,", he whispered. I watched the recognizable spin, the shot, the release…. "I understand you had a change of address…." *Swish.*

Cecil had a younger brother who was my age. Dennis was also known as Box, a moniker he'd earned given his boxing ability. And for that very reason, Box was never tested. When picking a fight with someone, a guy was far more likely to challenge someone called Showtime or Sugar Bear or even Loose Booty before a guy called Box. Box was thin and fast, and when he put a move on, he'd beat a guy clean and get a step. But instead of rocketing to the hoop, Box would put another move on back in the direction from which he just came and back into the trailing defender who'd just caught up by virtue of the reverse move, the sum of which significantly muted Box's success, but nevertheless fueled his spirit. He reveled in the moves and not the basket, so the outcome didn't particularly bother Box. His happy-go-lucky demeanor (and intimidating nickname) buoyed him, a perpetual song coming from his smiling lips. Song, however, was a relative term as Box was never bound by accurate lyrics or consistent songs for that matter. He frequently juxtaposed not only lyrics and melodies, but entire genres. For instance, he'd inadvertently join The 5th Dimension with the Temptations, singing, "Up, up, and away…on cloud nine."

Charlie Shell had no nickname. He was a six- foot -five - inch jumping jack who probably should have attended KHS, a prospect I never considered at the time; but in hindsight, I realize he would have made us one of the best teams in the nation. Instead, Shell attended Vianney High School, a Catholic school on the edge of Kirkwood. But as with all of us, Shell's high school had no bearing on events at the Center; he, as did I, found his skills acquiescent to the older, more established players. Still, Shell was the apple of Ricky Nelson's eye, because when Ricky missed—and Ricky missed a lot since he shot a lot—he wanted Charlie to pluck those rebounds and hand them back. So Ricky would shoot then instinctively shout, "Pull, Chollie!" to his big man before the shot even reached the rim.

With Ricky's cred and Charlie's inside presence, the two made a pretty dominant duo exceeded perhaps only by the Williams brothers. There were four Williamses, none of who bore much resemblance to the others except that each was an outstanding hoop player. The oldest brother Sam was a starting guard for St. Louis University, and although his appearances were rare, they were nonpareil. Sam was unguardable, squeezing off pinpoint jumpers against other guards, and streaking past embarrassed big men for layups, shots that one couldn't get to in time even to foul. And Sam never said a word. This was in stark contrast to brothers David and Robert, who spouted nonstop from the moment they entered clear through the moment they left. The middle Williams, Donnie, possessed a muscular physique and dour countenance setting a tone that required no words – a prototypical strong and silent type. Everyone feared Donnie excluding his brothers. The only reason that the Williams brothers didn't dominate at the Center was their competitiveness with each other. They'd often maneuver to avoid playing on the same team. This was especially true with David and Robert, who never played together, but never guarded each other either, an arrangement that enabled them to continually trash talk without ever settling a thing. David would drain a jumper and Robert would holler, "Who's got him?" The guilty defender would look Robert's way as though he might prefer to switch. "Don't make me come over there and guard him."

"Like you've got anything for me," David would snipe.

"I ain't gonna guard you, punk," Robert would quip. "This next one's off."

Distraction played a major part in Robert's game; he'd talk to his opponent, forcing him to miss even before shooting the ball. An opponent would pull up his dribble and Robert would stop, hands down, and chide, "That's off." And despite the shooter's clean look, he'd miss just because of the distraction. "Told you it was off."

All of these characters conjoined for those few hours in that one place where the game was simple and pure and insulated from the outside. I'm not sure when or how it happened, but one day when I entered, I realized that I'd come home. Each of us is a million different people, altered slightly by each person we meet and each space that we occupy. It is the feeling of self that governs our feelings toward others; my love or hate for a person stems from the love or hate I feel for myself when I'm with that person. The Center was comfortable and those players were real, and when I was there with them, I loved who I was.

81

After a few years, I'd earned my own cred as well as an interpretive guide, so when I'd walk out those doors, sweaty, fulfilled, and spent, the chatter was as clear as a bell.

"That's off."

"How do you know? I ain't even shot it yet."

"Then go ahead and shoot it. That's off!"

"Pull, Chollie!"

"Told you."

"Sweet Caroline…I can't get next to you…."

Chapter 5

We're in our 1–2–1–1 full-court press and we've got them rattled. They reach the frontcourt, but it's an effort, and when we drop into our 2–3 zone, we're just missing steals, and Rock bats one out of bounds. They have no penetration and settle for a twenty-footer by 52. It's off and I rebound, then in one motion, I'm flinging it ahead to Billy. He and Tommy have a two-on-one because Raytown's not back, but as I release it, I'm tangled up with 40. As they call the foul, he's looking at the ref like it's a bad call, and although I never talk out there, I find myself saying, "You're lucky they called it or we had a layup." I look at Geppetto and then down the court at Billy and Tommy, and then back at Geppetto. Did you see that? We were gone.

I raise my pistol and fire, and the free throw makes it 5–4, our first lead. Again, we press and this time Jesse jumps 22 and he rushes a pass that Rock easily steals. Tommy's got it and he's pushing it, and 22 has to foul him to prevent a layup. The first free throw misses and Tommy flings his arms in disgust. Second one's no good either, but our zone defense holds up. I rebound a miss and I've got Billy and Tommy running out, and this time, no one stops me, and they're off to the races, but Raytown's got four guys back. Damn!

I go to the line with less than two minutes to go and it's still just 5–4. Embarrassing, but I've got my stroke now. Bang! Bang! Both free throws make it 7–4. Raytown works around our zone, and 52 spots up at the free throw line, making a fifteen-footer. The boy is not shy about shooting. Rock's pissed because he dropped low on Stolle and gave that one up. He's muttering as we head down court. I step out from the low block and Billy gives it to me fifteen feet out on the left side. I square up and Stolle's there, but he's on his heels, afraid I'll drive. Mistake.

You never want to let a shooter make two in a row like Stolle did. My jumper makes it 9–6, but worse for them, that's seven straight points and I'm no longer even in this gym. That last shot came from our driveway in front of the wicker fence, Mitch's outstretched hand nothing more than a peep sight. Number 52 gets it in the same spot and starts to shoot, but Rock has his vengeance, leaping at him and forcing a travel. I'm only vaguely aware, though, because an assassin only sees his next target.

I pick and pop, and I'm shooting the return pass so quickly I don't even see the three Raytown players rushing because this one's from just inside the bushes on the Johnson's driveway, the one where I used to shovel snow so I could shoot Saturday mornings. It was a fair deal. They got free movement for their cars, and I got free reign across their bushes and patio and occasionally their kitchen windows. That rim was frozen and unforgiving, so I had to swish the shots just like I'm doing now. That makes nine straight, which by driveway rules is game over. It's funny how all those years spent shooting by myself on lonely, asphalt venues I'd imagined playing in The Game. Now, finally, here it is— I'm actually playing in The Game—only I'm finding myself right back in the driveway, back home alone in the game.

It's 11–6 and we're right on the verge of taking over. Geppetto's still waving his hands, but we've got his attention now.

They get a layup, and whether they meant to or not, Raytown just slowed the game again. Player 52 misses from the elbow and Stolle sneaks inside for the put back—his first hoop—and they're back within one as the quarter ends. They're better than I thought, but we've got three steals and they've made five turnovers, plus we've got a couple of deflections. Our defense is good; ten points yielded is fine. We've just got to shoot better. Mr. Miller doesn't have much to say. The problem's not our scheme; it's our execution. But last night in our semifinal, we were trailing by five after a quarter, and ran them off the floor in the second. Tonight, we played a crappy first quarter, but we're still leading. Time to turn up the gain.

Center jump and the ref throws it even further back over Stolle's head. He volleyballs it back to his guy. We like to run off the tip and that's twice we've been denied. It's a little thing, but in a game like this…First possession's theirs and they hit a jumper to retake the lead, 12–11. I hear the sound of a cement truck backing up to the court from behind their bench, and Geppetto rolls out the quicksand. For the next two minutes, we're pig wrestling in the muck, and I swear he'd just as soon go the rest of the game like this. But then Rhein Dabler, our six-foot-eight-inch man-mountain, grabs a rebound, holds it high with two hands over his head, outlets it to me, I dribble once at midcourt, kick ahead to Scott Markle, one dribble, and a layup. It's our first fast break score, and it's so quick and simple one would think it was nothing. But it was something. It's what we practiced every day, over and over and over. It's who we are and how we win and what we have to do to win. It's what opponents dread and scheme against and contort to prevent, but never quite can. It's what blew Carthage away in the second

85

quarter last night and what Geppetto surely told his guys to avoid at all costs. It's what Mr. Miller taught us to do.

Mr. Miller

Room gets suddenly still
And when you'd almost bet
You could hear yourself sweat, he walks in
Eyes black as coal
And when he lifts his face
Every ear in the place is on him
 –"Brother Love's Traveling Salvation Show,"
Neil Diamond

He was a teacher, after all, a math teacher. That's what he'd studied to become and that's the job that he found fulfilling. Coaching hoop was just another teaching job. So when Mr. Miller sat me down in the locker room that day before practice, it was the teacher who spoke.

"I think you're ready to play varsity basketball." His smoker's voice, burnt and charred, came deep from within his throat, but his face looked earnest and his eyes seemed filled with wisdom, such that his students looked at him without looking away, listening, even as teenagers in a hurry.

"Normally I wouldn't try something like this," he continued, leaning forward, putting his elbows on his knees, "but we need someone to fill in at forward and right now no one is getting it done. This might be rushing you before you're ready, but you'd have come up next year and this will give you some experience."

It was like listening to a teacher map out a problem and then listening to him solve it. I said nothing and he didn't wait for a reply. "I talked to your parents and they said it was OK with them." I thought to myself, "Why would they object?" The switch would give them more games to watch, but it would wipe out my free time before baseball started. "What I'd like for you to do is work out with us today, then go home, and talk it over with your folks tonight."

"OK." And that's all I said. I slowly returned to dressing, giving Mr. Miller an opportunity to precede me out to practice. I'd already encountered the resentment of the sophomores, so I was imagining how the varsity would react to Mr. Miller walking his new pet player into their practice.

A few minutes later, I walked out and Mr. Miller was speaking to them. Judging by the sudden, silent stares, he'd just told them that the skinny freshman would be joining them. I felt out of place. It was like those dreams where you're in a classroom and you realize that you're in your pajamas and you haven't studied for the day's test, and you think, "Damn! How did I get all the way here before I noticed my jammies and what the hell was I doing when I should have been studying?"

"OK, Rogers, you're in for Doty." I didn't know who Doty was, but I assumed he was the one who'd just walked off. "Let's just pass and pick away. Rogers at the free throw line and pick down for Farrell." Hold it. I knew that Farrell was the star senior forward, but I didn't know who he was either, since the only time I'd gone to a varsity game that year I'd been chasing girls in the upper deck. I never watched a second of the game. After that first B team game, I spent my time pondering our failed getaway; after the last one, I went home to study for a test without watching the varsity. I scanned my new teammates. I glanced at Cecil, who instantly seemed to know my predicament and committed himself to offering no help. By process of elimination I knew Cecil wasn't Farrell and neither was I. Cecil triggered the play with a pass to the wing, so the wing wasn't Farrell either. I stepped down the lane in the general direction of both big men, and one popped to the free throw line so it was a marginal pick but a positive ID.

Two nights later, my father dropped me off in a parking lot filling with cars driven by my older teammates, where I lugged my newly assigned leather, varsity gym bag into the sparsely filled KHS gym, and sat in the bleachers. I watched as the B team continued its lonely quest for success, seeing Tommy and my fellow freshmen grow before my eyes. When the rest of the varsity abandoned their seats to go dress for the game, I followed, and when we burst through the paper banner onto the court, the band was playing, the stands were full, and I was warming up with men. I took a seat on the bench when the game began, and halfway through the first quarter, Mr. Miller waved me into the game. Cecil came out as I went in, and as he passed by, he grinned at the floor and whispered, "Young Boy."

The home crowd stood and my new teammates paused, hands on hips as I nervously trotted onto the floor. This same group had finished third in state the previous year and many

88

believed they were one player away from charting a return course. But it wasn't just any player they needed. Rather it was last year's All-State forward, Petey Thornton, and his twenty-four points per game scoring average. What they got instead was me. Petey was the number one player in the state of Missouri the previous year and went on to play major college ball. I knew of his exploits from listening to the broadcast of Kirkwood's semifinal loss to Columbia Hickman and from seeing newspaper pictures of him out-jumping taller players and rolling up nearly seven hundred points his senior year. But he was more than a great player. Petey was the first real black star for Kirkwood and one of the first for any local high school team outside of the Public High League.

Basketball was still a predominantly white sport in the sixties right up until 1966 when Texas Western won the NCAA championship with five black starters, defeating all-white Kentucky and its blatantly bigoted head coach, Adolph Rupp. One resentful white observer rationalized that Texas Western team's win as follows: "They can do everything with the basketball but sign it." That was the state of hoops when Petey Thornton played. Playing in the mostly white Suburban South Conference, Petey was subjected to racial slurs by opposing crowds, biased calls by officials, and aggressive acts by opponents. Mr. Miller took it upon himself to encourage Petey's play as well as to monitor Petey's comportment, once again teaching lessons not just to Petey but to his teammates, his schoolmates, and ultimately to the entire St. Louis area, not as a mission or a movement, but simply as a mentor.

I stepped into Petey's world as a raw freshman with only a handful of formal games under my belt and no real varsity knowledge, since I'd not even watched the games. But with high-scoring forward Dave Farrell and freewheeling guard Bob Carson providing the senior leadership, they weren't looking for points; they were looking for hustle and rebounding, neither of which required experience. So I ran around like a banshee and started grabbing rebounds by the handful. I knew better than to shoot except after a rebound, and even so, I scored six points that first game followed by eleven and then thirteen. We ended the season on a healthy winning streak including each of the three games in which I played. We'd be facing archrival Webster Groves in the first round of the state regionals.

Because my junior high school was separate from Kirkwood High, there existed a natural division between my hoop fortunes and life as a ninth grade student. Once our junior high hoop season ended, student life moved on with cheerleaders attending track meets and students returning to their various stations at the Quick Shop or Burger King off campus. My ventures over to the high school and adventures on the court were conveniently left off of everyone else's radar screen, which was exactly the way I wanted it. Sports in general and hoop in particular had always been a private passion for me, a retreat from classwork and social situations that felt so foreign. I was on the verge of putting my ascension behind me without so much as a nod from my fellow freshmen.

Until the day of the regional game, that is. As I walked between classes that morning, I was the subject of pointing and covered-mouth giggles and guffaws, none of which made any sense until I walked past the administration office and there, spanning a good eight feet, was pasted a sign: "Good luck, Drew!" Constructed and hung by well-meaning Pep Club members, it proclaimed their well wishes, but struck a nervous chord in me. This was my first experience with the intrusion of The Game into the game. I dropped my head and hoped Mrs. Parham wouldn't take issue with my sign defiling her wall.

Webster was the second ranked team in the state that night. They were heavily favored to beat Kirkwood and win the regional, which was being played on their home court. I lacked much rapport with any of these car-driving, girlfriend-bearing, sideburn-wearing, eighteen year olds, but in the visitor's locker room that night, Farrell took me aside and told me that the next loss would be his last high school game. He had no intention of losing. "Just do what you've been doing," he said. "We'll take care of the rest." Fellow senior leader Bob Carson slapped me on the shoulder and I followed them onto the floor determined to just do what I do.

And then I saw my "Good luck, Drew!" sign pasted along the far wall behind Webster's basket. Rather, we all saw it at once. It was trailing me like toilet paper stuck to a shoe. Farrell looked at me like, "What the hell is that?" Carson wouldn't look at me at all. The game commenced and I entered at my customary juncture, halfway through the first quarter, taking my position in the lane for a free throw, standing next to a Webster big man. "Are you Drew?" he asked, just a little too animated. I stared holes into my sneakers and nodded slightly. "Well," he bellowed, arching his back and putting his hands on his hips. "Then good luck, Drew!"

That sign held up better than we did, lasting the entire game in one piece while we unraveled in the second half and succumbed to Webster, 72–59. I sat in the locker room watching Farrell and Carson change out of those wretched, worn, little KHS uniforms, the ones that looked like Hanes underwear with red piping and tiny numbers. I watched them stare at those corny cotton outfits and stuff them away in their bags like they were abandoning their very souls and I felt ashamed. I felt ashamed by my addition to their team, my game minutes, my very presence on the floor with them that night and, ultimately, by my sign. I was supposed to elevate them, to carry them forward, if not to the state final four as Petey Thornton had done, then at least several rounds deep in the regionals, and certainly not to a double-digit loss in round one.

But these were men. "Hurry up, boys. Let's go." That's all Mr. Miller had to say. The next regional game had started, our season already a memory. Thirty painfully silent minutes later, our bus pulled into the KHS parking lot and Mr. Miller stood and spoke. "There's not much to say. We'll meet at 3:15 tomorrow in my classroom to wrap things up."

Denver Miller was the decorated dean of basketball coaches by virtue of his eventual forty-three years coaching Kirkwood hoop and seven hundred and ninety wins. He'd taken a score of teams deep into the state tournament, several of which could have or should have won it all, but none had. He was an analytical assessor and manipulator of players and teams, a skill befitting a math teacher as each season and each match-up formed an equation needing to be solved. To fans and to writers, he was an icon. To many players, he was a father figure, a drill sergeant, or a psychiatrist. To my father, at first glance at least, he was a bellicose, overwhelmed, and under-qualified old man.

By promoting me to varsity, Mr. Miller may have gained my father's permission, but he failed to gain his respect. As my father sat in the stands for those first varsity games, he watched Mr. Miller, balding and red-faced, spreading out his feet, lashing out at officials, complaining to his assistant coaches, hollering at and occasionally berating his players, and generally carrying on in extreme volatility. He appeared in stark contrast to my freshman coach, the B team coach, and most significantly to the young, composed opposing varsity coaches. To his credit, my father never shared his opinions with me, because like most fathers in that era, he eschewed the enlistment of his kids as friends or confidants.

So I had no idea that the summer following my freshman year, he succumbed to the pull of more modern schools and gyms like Parkway and Lindbergh and Mehlville, and paid visits to coaches Lou Lorch and Irv Leimer to investigate their programs. He even looked at houses in the Lindbergh district. What I did know was that the next season, immediately following a thrashing at the hands of a very talented and well-coached Lindbergh bunch, my father sat at the dinner table and asked me if I'd like to go play for Lindbergh. I looked over at him, across an unidentifiable and equally indigestible casserole, a minimum number of obligatory bites of which stood between me and dessert, and said simply, "No, thanks." Why not? "Because I want to play with my friends." I didn't give it a second thought, but he did. And years later, after I'd played almost ninety games for Denver Miller, my father gave stark admission to the fact that jumping to another school and another coach would have been the biggest mistake he could have made regarding my hoop fortunes and my growth as a young man.

As his career reached its late stages, Miller was feted, once upon coaching his one thousandth game and again shortly after achieving his seven hundredth victory. As part of his living legend, certain qualities were bestowed upon him like omniscience, omnipotence, and sainthood. But that's not who he was and those weren't the reasons he was so successful. Those certainly weren't the reasons why I was so lucky to have continued playing for him despite the lure of younger, flashier coaches.

Mr. Miller was a teacher, yes, but to be more precise, he was an analyst and an architect, traits that he complemented with a knowledge so broad and diverse that in the span of just four years—from my senior year to my younger brother's junior year—his teams evolved from our full-court press, run-and-gun style to the slow down four corners delay game that the University of North Carolina popularized in the days before a shot clock. And he made those refinements based on the players on hand, from the stable of racehorses my year to the less athletic, guard-oriented four corners group. Some coaches develop a system and then impose it, forcing it down to junior high and grade school so that when players reach high school, they know the system and have already adapted to it. Mr. Miller knew every system and he could teach them all, but like a sculptor, he would fashion a system from the materials he was given, producing magnificent works of art, each unique and adapted to its parts. And this brought success. After taking fast break teams to the state final two straight years, he took his slow-down, four-corners team to within a last second, half-court heave of returning to the Final Four. He was equal parts Picasso and Einstein, plus a little junkyard dog. I doubt Picasso or Einstein were ever seen barking at their works the way that Mr. Miller occasionally barked at his.

At the heart of his success lay a system, a mathematical scoring of each player's contributions, game by game, assigning points to made shots, rebounds, and assists, while subtracting points for things like turnovers and missed shots. He scored each player in each game and posted a summary sheet at practice the day after. Most of us hung on those postings like prisoners hoping for a pardon. You may have scored a bunch of points in the game, but if you missed too many shots in the process, you got a low grade. You knew it and he knew it, and not much else mattered. This system was also a means for Mr. Miller to make objective decisions about who played and who would take the shots.

Art and science each have their limits, however. The year before he began running our horses and then stabling his four corners crew, Mr. Miller took a look at the varsity my sophomore year. He must have been tempted to turn and run.

95

The materials he assembled for that year were a challenge even to one as intrepid as he. There were two seniors and a whole bunch of sophomores, with very little in between. So his approach consisted of stirring the pot, testing various combinations, and then teaching and conditioning players for the future. Tommy and I led the group of five sophomores and both of us were in the starting lineup to begin the season. Bill Tice put aside his bear hunting long enough to start for the team as did returning seniors Cecil Jones and Jim Doty. Mr. Miller established roles for the two seniors as leaders and facilitators, bridges to the sophomores' promising futures. Doty readily accepted his role, but Cecil did not.

Kirkwood's cross country team was number one in the nation that year and Cecil was co-captain of that team, gaining individual honors as the tenth rated runner in the state and fifteenth in the nation. He was a hard worker, a gifted athlete, and a senior who was acutely aware that this basketball season would be his last. The shots he took and the points he scored were finite and dwindling. Mr. Miller's tedious effort to build for the future conflicted directly with Cecil's last hurrah.

We were en route to a 6–15 record along with a lot of frustration. Senior substitute Brian Carter, a fast, strong, black football player recruited to basketball for his athleticism, had to be asking himself why Mr. Miller had solicited his participation and then played him so sparingly. This came to a head shortly before Christmas during a duck walk drill when Carter asked what the hell we were doing. As the fourteen of us moved in a giant circle, down on our haunches in the name of conditioning (and one or two players quacking in derision), Carter challenged the drill. We all heard him and we all stopped.

"All right boys, everybody up." Mr. Miller glowered as we assembled before him.

"Boys?" carped Carter. And there it was, the race card, hanging like a day-old balloon, too hackneyed to rise, and too topical to disappear, bobbing between Coach and Carter. Mr. Miller stared disgustedly at Carter who stared at the floor.

"Well you're not girls are you?"

Several of us giggled and I caught Cecil shaking his head and stifling a grin. No, we were not girls, we were boys, boys surrounded by racial issues, led by a coach trying to teach, and all of us just wanting to work and play and grow. Carter hadn't meant anything by his comment; he was just sick of duck walking, losing, and riding the bench. I was pretty sick of those first two issues myself.

Coincidentally or not, Carter got more playing time after that, and I liked having those football shoulders at my side playing against bigger and more mature players. Carter was also good for one piece of sage advice: "We do NOT want to lose the first game in the Normandy Christmas tournament." Why not? "Because that means we're practicing that whole week between Christmas and New Year's instead of playing more games." Now that was senior leadership. Carter's words proved to be more premonition than precaution. We got drilled in our first round game by St. Louis University High School (SLUH) 59–33, but it wasn't just that we got beat; it was how we got beat.

Dennis "Box" Jones had earned a spot on the varsity team as our fifth sophomore through a series of dazzling dribbling displays in preseason practices. Although Tommy and Cecil were our starting guards, they had a hard time staying with Box in practice, a point of both pride and frustration for older brother Cecil. Box would bust a double move and glide away from the two of them, smiling and singing his jumbled songs.

The SLUH game was an early morning affair at Normandy and we were sleepwalking from the opening tip. A sleepy SLUH team struggled to awaken right along with us, so it was still close at the start of the second half. And that's when SLUH put on its full-court zone press. It was our first experience with a press. Up until then, a press had meant merely the fifteen or twenty minutes of practice spent preparing for one, resulting in critical ignorance and naiveté. Three aborted inbounds attempts later, we were huddled around Mr. Miller trying to remember what those damn press-break sequences were, with the SLUH lead now double digits, and Carter hissing about the weeks' worth of practices that he wouldn't abide. So Mr. Miller called on Box. It kind of figured, really. If your team can't pass it up court, give it to your best dribbler and turn him loose. I took the ball out and glanced at Box as we lined up. His lips curled into a smile. "I second that emotion," he mimed joyfully. He broke and I got it to him as he wheeled up court, hammering the ball and sailing past the first defender. "Wow," I thought. A second defender slid over, trapping him against the sideline, and when Box turned, that first defender arrived, forcing him to pick

98

up his dribble. Box held it over his head looking for help, but the four of us were still thrashing through our playbooks, wishing we'd paid more attention during those drills. As I mentally concluded that Box's next song should be "Ball of Confusion," SLUH knocked it loose and went by me so fast I couldn't even contest the layup.

So I inbounded it again and Box was done singing, was done smiling, and was done getting stripped by a bunch of white guys. So as he gathered in my pass, his eyes appeared yellow and he steamed with frustration, and this time when he turned, he led with an elbow that just missed the first guard or it would've crushed the guy's head like a tin can. Box dribbled up court with his head up, but he wasn't looking to pass, he was looking to retaliate, and when that second guard got there, Box had another elbow locked and loaded. That one found its mark right in the guy's chest, but Box was clever. He was going the other way before the guy could wince or the ref could call a foul. Box was still on the sideline when a third player cut him off, and damn if that first one didn't stay with it, doggedly trailing Box. Sure enough, when Box backed up, that first guy reached in and stole the ball clean. Then it was a jailbreak as three of them bore down on me and I wasn't asking where the rest of my guys had gone because they were up court, still rifling that playbook in total disarray, but I had a fast break to contest and—oh yeah, that's another thing we'd never worked on—so I moved toward the dribbler and two quick passes led to an easy layup as I stood inert, tied in knots by the invisible string behind those passes, and just before the guy put it in, Box flashed by him swinging a haymaker that missed only because those guys were too quick to even punch.

The ref stopped the game to warn Box (even though Box didn't connect) for bad intentions, I guess. I took it out, but there was no third time, no charm. Box barreled into their guard, fists balled up at his side and a vicious snarl of smack talk thrust in his face, and the SLUH guy laughed right back. Box saw that the other one was laughing too and suddenly Box became the Tasmanian Devil, everything in his path uprooted and flying. And then, just like that, he was gone.

So what had been an ignominious (and short-lived) debut for Box became a major lesson learned for me—actually, several lessons. First, it takes team movement to beat a zone press. Second, it's better to press than be pressed. Third, a team can stop a single dribbler just about every time, removing his smile and muting his singing career. Oh, and one more tip: don't lose your first round game at the Normandy tournament because that Christmas week of practices is awful. But despite our travails, we improved in the second half of the season. I won't say we gelled or came together because the gap between seniors and sophomores was too much—at least for those particular seniors and sophomores. And we were still losing. Failure and frustration are fertile grounds for outside agendas like race and ego.

I emerged as the team's leading scorer, averaging about sixteen points a game. Cecil was up and down, scoring a dozen or more points one game and then less than half that the next. Our motion offense was designed to provide Cecil space to shoot or pass, depending on how defenses reacted, and more often than not, Cecil drew defenders leaving other players like me wide open. Practices increasingly digressed into discussions between Cecil and Mr. Miller about the necessity and advisability of passing to me, talks which at one point drew to a standstill after Cecil was instructed to pass me the ball.

"Hell, I'm wide open here. Why am I passing him the ball?"

"Because he's shooting 55 percent and you're shooting 35 percent, dammit. Pass him the ball." Those figures came right off Mr. Miller's score sheets, plain as day and 100 percent objective. I caught the look in Cecil's eyes, one of contrition but not abdication.

Two nights later, we played at Parkway Central, a team that blew us out months before and was vying for the Suburban South title. But we had improved and proceeded to match Parkway basket for basket all the way. With two minutes to play, we called time-out trailing by one, and I felt particularly motivated because Parkway's senior center, Mike Pratt, had just bounced a pass between my outspread legs to a cutting teammate for a layup.

Mr. Miller drew up the play: a simple pick for Cecil to dribble right and pass down to me on the baseline, the same pass, in fact, that Cecil had challenged in practice. Cecil dribbled, I flashed, he hit me, and I delivered some Mike Pratt payback, putting us in the lead for the first time all night. Parkway responded and we called time-out again, trailing by one with a minute to play. Mr. Miller called the same play. We inbounded and I set up along the baseline while Cecil dribbled right. Pratt had his back to Doty as he moved down to pick for me, and it became obvious that I was going to open up again. I was already licking my fingers since I planned to catch and shoot in one motion, and then I'd stare Pratt down the whole way as we ran up court.

With one last look at Cecil, I flashed and the whole scene turned blurry. Everything…slowed…down. Cecil came off his pick in slow motion and my hands were like lead as I raised them to receive the pass. "Heeeeee's oooooopen." Mr. Miller's voice sounded like a 45 RPM record playing at 33 speed. Cecil's eyes met mine, a long, steadfast gaze, and behind him, the Parkway gym evaporated. At once, we were in the Center with Loose Booty setting the pick. Cecil held my gaze as he brought the ball up with both hands and there it was—his kick step—so I knew what was coming and I knew what I was supposed to do. I shoved Pratt as I turned to rebound and squeezed by him into the lane.

Cecil didn't run the play. He broke it off to shoot instead. If one didn't know better, they'd think that Cecil was selfish or cocky or a racist and couldn't stand to throw it to a white guy, especially some sophomore. One might even be tempted to say that it was Cecil's last hurrah and Young Boy had two more years, so what the hell. But the simple fact was that it was all part of the game, Cecil against the Parkway defender. Cecil was a shooter and shooters shoot the ball. And they send Young Boys off to rebound. The Game was irrelevant as always and so was whatever play some coach drew up. Cecil tossed me

102

a bone on that first one, but that next shot was going up, a better shot in his opinion than any shot he envisioned me taking. All the paper said the next day was that Kirkwood lost by three. Cecil made that shot to put us ahead one last time before losing, but when he boarded the bus, he was animated and engaged. "One more look, that's all I needed," he panted. "I had that boy set up. I was gonna cross over on him and get that free throw line jumper. I *had* him!"

Ours was a young team. When the regionals arrived, we grew even younger, pulling sophomores Jesse Jackson and Sam Weaver up to the varsity giving us seven sophomores total. We won our first regional game, drawing as our second round opponent undefeated Suburban South champion Lindbergh High and its dynamic senior duo Steve Blind and Gary Link. One measure of coaching success is how one's team fares against the same opponent over the course of a season. We'd lost to Lindbergh by twenty-two and twenty-four points during the regular season. In spite of the duck walk protest and the Box meltdown, we'd grown as a team and Mr. Miller had instilled in us basic tenets like defending and playing hard. When we took the floor against Lindbergh, we had nothing to lose.

I grew up that night. A lot of us did. We swarmed Lindbergh, stealing the ball and forcing them into bad shots. We were conservative on offense, protecting the ball and patiently working for good shots. We took an early lead and held it throughout the first half; Lindbergh's crowd growing ever more silent as their players began to cast nervous glances at one another. They were state champion contenders and we were cannon fodder, but we had a hold of them like rabid dogs and we wouldn't let go. Doty fed me for a layup as the first half ended to give us a 28–23 lead. I had fifteen points and we had them with just sixteen minutes to go.

The next morning, the paper read that Lindbergh blew Kirkwood away in that second half, ending our season and eventually propelling Lindbergh to the Final Four. But we were better than they were for a half. Mr. Miller was quoted as saying, "If we could have scored a bucket or two at the start of the third quarter, I think we might have had a shot at them." I felt the same way. We had come out tentative, lost the lead, and couldn't contain them like a failing seawall beneath a crushing tide. For the second straight year, my season ended in a regional loss in the Webster Groves gym, but there had been redemption with each finish. My freshman year, I got a taste of varsity hoop and playing with the big boys. My sophomore year, we won our first round game and I witnessed the growth among our sophomore group as we all realized our future potential and Mr. Miller's wisdom.

As that first half ended and my layup fell in, Doty and I stood staring at the scoreboard and then at each other and we locked in an embrace of incredulity and euphoria. I thought about that moment and that feeling for an eternity, long after Doty and Cecil faded away and followed their own futures. The bus ride home was quiet, but it was not forlorn. We had beaten a great team for a half and seven of us still had two more years ahead of us. Tommy and Jesse and I sat quietly in the sway of the old bus, streetlights casting dim shadows that darted across our young, earnest faces. Three pieces in place. Three lumps of clay in the hands of a master sculptor. Two more to go.

Denver Miller, impatient. "Get it out and go!"

Chapter 6

Billy's stepping up. He nails an eighteen-footer to put us up two, then he jumps over to press the ball. He's loving this. Every morning, the two of us start talking hoops after study hall, continue while dressing for practice, on the court, on bus rides to games, and on Saturday mornings when running the scoreboard for JV games. There was a picture in the paper of Kevin Joyce of South Carolina standing with the ball under his arm, stalling until the opponents come out of their zone. There's no shot clock, so the team that's trailing has to come out and play the ball. We figure someone will do that to us someday—sit back in a zone when we're leading—and we debate which of us would be the one to stand out there like Joyce, controlling the game and the photo op. Either way, we'll be ready for that moment.

We're up three with five minutes to go in the second quarter. It's still their pace, but we're bigger and better and slowly we're gaining leverage. They call time-out and we've gathered around Mr. Miller like so many puppies at a mother's teat. Geppetto's got his starting five around him and the rest are banished to the bench like tardy school kids. Geppetto's scribbling on his clipboard and hollering at each of his guys. Something's up. They inbound against our press, make the frontcourt, and size up our zone, then they begin to play catch around the perimeter and across the top of the key. There it is—they're stalling.

106

Billy takes one look and sits back at the top of our zone, his head jerking back and forth like a spectator at a tennis match, back and forth, back and forth. He stays crouched, hands at his sides, and steals a glance at the ref. Billy knows the rule. The trailing team must initiate play whether on offense or defense. You can't stand out there with the ball under your arm or send it back and forth if you're behind. Five seconds and it's a T, one free throw for us plus possession. One…two…

Our other guard, Scott Markle, jumps out to contest a pass. The ref stops his count. Billy hollers for Scott to retreat, but we've never practiced sitting back. We challenge everything. That's why our practices are dogfights, oftentimes chippier than games. Scott's out there again, contesting, scrapping. Billy waves him back, his arm flapping like a one-winged bird struggling to get altitude. One…two…Scott jumps out again. He just can't help it, it's instinct now, what he's been drilled to do. Billy jabs a finger at him like Mrs. Parham right before she writes a yellow slip. Jesse steps up behind Billy and shoves him to go out and play the ball, and now he gets the yellow slip finger jab, and just to be sure, Billy turns and points at all of us. "Stay back!"

Incredibly, Dabler darts up from the baseline and shoves Scott forward. That's a 235 pound shove and Scott goes out. It's comical. Raytown has run thirty seconds off the clock while we kibitz. Billy puts his hands on his hips, takes a deep breath, and slides over next to Scott. Whatever Billy barks through the din seems to get through. Scott drops back, tail between his legs, watching those two guys throw his dinner back and forth.

Geppetto has to know the rule, doesn't he? This is going to be a free throw and possession to us. What's he thinking? Well, he just wiped out one minute of game time, gone forever, and when they call the technical I brick the free throw, so he's gotten just what he bargained for. What happened to that sniper's touch of mine? Ten minutes of hibernation and boredom. I could've shoveled the Johnson's whole driveway in less time than it's been between shots.

But Billy's in charge, that little chess match sparking his competitive fire. He dribbles to the right side and calls one for me. Dabler and Jesse double pick on the block, and I'm popping out along the baseline. He puts it right there and I don't even have to move my feet. Face up, and I bury that fifteen-footer, just like in Bad Dude Carnahan's driveway. We're up five again and now Billy's in overdrive, sliding across the top of our zone and moving Scott around, too, so the two of them become twin branches, sweeping in and out, clearing out anything in their path.

Dabler jumps a shooter who travels, we miss, and next time down, we force a bad pass—it sails out to midcourt and into the scorers' table. Billy's over there, grabbing it away from the radio announcer, and handing it to the official, taking it and putting it into play in a blur. We miss a couple, but Billy's pushing the pace. He goes to the line and makes two, and once again our lead is five, 20–15. I miss one from the left side, the one from in front of the wicker fence, but I'm not worried. Billy's running things and making shots, and like the circus guy making the balloon animals, he's got his hands on all of us, shaping us with squeaky twists, and putting the carnival into motion.

The Thrill

As the present now
Will later be past
The order is rapidly fadin'
And the first one now will later be last
For the times they are a-changin'
　　　－"The Times They Are A-Changin'," Bob Dylan

Kirkwood basketball games in the midsixties were a series of episodes of boys behaving badly. Senior guard Jim Moulder was white and sophomore guard Bob Pace was black. Both were shooters, serious trigger-happy, gun-toting, rapid fire marauders whose legs could be chopped off and torsos could be ravaged, but with a single-minded resolve so strong that as long as they had the strength to lift their arms and line it up, they'd squeeze off another round. They might miss and miss and miss, but that next one was going in. They were rival pirates to whom the word *share* referenced their portion of the booty—hoarding rather than distributing. They made Cecil Jones look tame.

In an early season game, Pace broke free down court as Moulder dribbled. Moulder saw him, ignored him, and brought the ball up to shoot it himself. Mr. Miller challenged him after the game, asking why he hadn't thrown ahead to a wide-open Pace. "Because he wouldn't have thrown it to me." Mr. Miller pondered Moulder's response briefly and admitted that he'd had past players with the same attitude, but Moulder was the first to admit as such aloud.

The season dragged on with each player refusing to pass. It got to the point that when the opposing team scored, Pace and Moulder would step inbounds, insisting that someone else take it out, while the ball would bounce idly, *patter, patter, patter*. Each guy knew that if he threw it in, he'd never get it back. Those among the sparse crowd witnessing this selfishness and Mr. Miller's resultant harangues might have wondered what the hell was going on. Moulder's younger brother, Bill, was there every game, pressing forward in his seat and yearning for the days when he would play high school ball—sharing rather than hording his share, so that the coach would be able to sit and enjoy things rather than holler and manage.

It would be six or seven years before that happened, several years spent playing hoops with his older brother in the backyard, getting worked, bullied, beat up, and teased, all standard little brother fare. Bill never won a game—ever. Jim wouldn't throw him so much as a morsel of hope. Bill had two choices then: quit or persevere. After each thrashing, after his older brother tired of the massacre and split, Bill would remain, dribbling and shooting, tirelessly working toward the only goal he could imagine: redemption. Sometimes mixing hopelessness with a strong work ethic results in overachievement. As a young boy, it seemed to Bill that he was never good enough. He was always fighting for a position, fighting for playing time, fighting for success. But he never showed concern. The driveway beat-downs inured him because the only thing worse than losing was humiliation; though he had no control over the outcome, he sure as hell could control his demeanor. Like a duck paddling

110

furiously below water who appears to glide from above, Bill assumed a swagger, a strut, a façade designed to play with an opponent's mind while masking his own intense fear of failure.

Bill Moulder was that player who, if he was on your team, you loved him, and if he was on the other team, you hated him. I first encountered him in little league baseball when I was about ten. And I hated him. He was a feisty left-handed pitcher and he'd already mastered the strut, the stare, and worst of all, command of an off-speed hook that nobody our age could hit. So Bill would flap around on the mound bedeviling hitters, and we'd strike out and practically sprint back to the dugout. Bill didn't throw that hard, so after we'd seen him once, we figured we'd murder him the next time and the next and the time after that. I didn't know Bill or anything about him except that I was going to hit that damn curve ball the next time he spun one in.

Because Bill was a year younger, our teams didn't match up again for a few years, but when they did, we were both older and the outfield fences were tempting if not altogether reachable. This meant that when Bill started serving up those yackers, we practically came out of our cleats lunging and flailing at them, so sure and so determined to pound one over the fence thereby stripping away his strut. Even as we'd trudge back to the dugout, we still felt convinced that we could hit him. But we never did.

Bill attended Lutheran elementary school while I attended public school, so our paths didn't cross again until my sophomore year in high school. Through sheer determination, hard work, and a number of basketball camps, he had grown

111

from older brother Jim's prey into an outstanding hoop player. Bill played in the Lutheran South school system, one that boasted a top-level basketball program. If the high school coaches had reached out to him, Bill would have stayed, but they didn't. Didn't they want him? Wasn't he good enough? He'd seen my freshman team play, and attracted by our success, he transferred to North Junior High his freshman year. And like the moon's gravitational pull on the tides, Bill's transfer shifted the balance of hoop power in Kirkwood's direction.

While our high school hoop team struggled through my sophomore season, I heard that North was on a roll with Bill Moulder as their leader. I remembered him and his bedeviling curve ball, but he played hoop? I had to go check that out. Bill was the real deal. At a time before point guard was even a position, Bill played the point, dominating the offense with the ball in his hand, driving, dishing, and shooting, as well as orchestrating the defense, while hounding the opposing ball handler into mistakes and frustration. I recognized the strut and the stare, both still cloaking his hidden fear. I found Bill fun to watch, but irrelevant. We had our hands full up at the high school that season, and North Junior High and Bill Moulder seemed a million miles away. I didn't realize that he was the same type of player that SLUH had used to press us out of the Normandy Tournament—technique and determination trumping raw athleticism.

But Mr. Miller knew. He'd steal over to those junior high games to study and ponder and plan. Tommy Grice had emerged as a solid guard even as Box flamed out and Cecil

112

graduated. This cocky white kid could very well join the show, maybe even run it. But first, he'd have to make the varsity team. That next fall, my junior year, while I was out on the football field, hoop practice began with the pace and fury of a war zone. During class, I'd hear rumors of the ferocity and see tiny snippets of evidence, a player limping down the hall, random bruises, black eyes. Once, when football practice ended early, I peeked inside the gym for the final few minutes of hoop practice to watch them scrimmage. Mr. Miller stalked up and down chewing his whistle and exhorting everyone to run, run, run. When the ball went out of bounds, he hollered to get it in and go. Defenders pressed every dribble, contested every pass, while the offense streaked up court. As the top returning scorer, I figured we'd be walking it up and pounding it inside to me, but their pace was dead opposite. It was clear that by the time I could post up inside, this group would already be gone. I turned and headed back down to the track to run extra sprints, something I started to do after every football practice in anticipation of the new basketball regimen.

Bill was a man possessed on the court. He'd been invited to practice with the varsity team while a determination was made as to where he belonged, varsity or B team. He'd watched us play that previous year, and despite our struggles, he counted at least four returning guards ahead of him: juniors Tommy, Box, and John Breimeier, as well as smooth senior Randy Vaughn. Amidst all that motion and activity, Bill still stood out, diving for loose balls and chasing down fast breaks after everyone else had given up. The sculptor had not yet chosen his

113

creation. He was squeezing the clay, eyeing various forms, searching for his masterpiece. At some point, Mr. Miller determined that not only would Bill join the mix, he would define it. By the time football ended and I joined the basketball group for my one week of practice before our first game, the commitment had been made that we would press up on defense and run like wolves on offense.

And what about my anticipation of being fed in the low post? After my senior season, Mr. Miller gave me all the recruiting letters he'd received from colleges inquiring about me. In the middle of the stack, I discovered an evaluation sheet that he'd completed for one of the schools. Shockingly, he had rated me an average jumper and an average shooter. What? The only area he rated me outstanding was transition, offense to defense and defense to offense. In essence, he'd said that in set situations I was average, but I could really get up and down the floor for my size. In hindsight, he was exactly right. And the scheme he devised for our team was perfect.

Coach ran my legs off that week in practice, and we took the floor for a first-round game in a four-team tournament at Maplewood High. The previous year, I'd been schooled by Tom McEvoy, a crafty senior center who head-faked me off my feet to go to the rim or create space for pull up jumpers en route to a tournament MVP performance and team championship. What a difference a year had made. This time, I was in charge, scoring at will while my team stayed in command. After a late charge by our opponents forced the game into overtime, we lost by a point, but we played well. I ended the game with twenty-four points.

As a sophomore playing in his first varsity game, Bill had twenty-five points off the bench.

They brought him off the bench because of his energy. Tommy and Vaughn started at guard. Vaughn was a tall, smooth shooter who kept teams honest with his outside shot. But when Bill entered the game, everything changed. He'd answer Mr. Miller's summons, rising slowly from the bench, tantalizing tugs at his warm-up snaps like a stripper building anticipation. He'd mosey to the scorers' table to report in and kneel, waiting for a stoppage, eyeing the play in front of him, his eyes darting mischievously. He looked every bit the chastened kid in the corner, who, rather than apologizing for his last act, is busy contriving his next.

Out on the floor, we'd see him squatting there and know to catch our breath to get ready—ready to sprint, ready to dive, and ready to pounce. He injected life into our press and chaos upon other teams, providing value beyond the points he scored and the plays he made, elevating our whole team's play. He fulfilled the exact image that Mr. Miller had sketched. Bill was more than the prototypical 'coach on the floor'; most times he ran it better, pushed it further, and built it more beautifully than even his sculptor had envisioned. He was Bill the Thrill.

Still, we remained young. For every steal or layup, there were turnovers and misses. Mr. Miller knew he wanted us to press, but he hadn't yet determined which press or which players. He used his point system to grade players and to determine the next game's starting lineup. We split our first two games at the Maplewood tournament and then we lost at home to Charlie Shell and Vianney. After a ton of preseason press heralding that year to be Kirkwood's, plus early season anticipation among the students (though thankfully no "Good luck, Drew!" signs), everyone wondered what was wrong. One senior student stopped me in the hall and said, "I thought you guys were supposed to be good this year." So had I. But it wasn't that simple. It wasn't about being good or bad, at least not yet. It was about learning who we were. There was a lot of change afoot and many moving parts. Our development into a pressure defense and fast break offense took time along with the integration of new players, first Bill and then the Williams brothers.

Donnie and Robert Williams transferred to Kirkwood that year from nearby Valley Park High, where their older brother, David, remained for his senior year, averaging nearly thirty points a game. Sophomore Robert was ineligible for the fall semester as he aligned his class credits. Junior Donnie suited up from the start. Donnie was an enigma, his deep black skin and muscular physique intimidating teammates and opponents alike. He was strong and fast and tough—a good hoop player, but mostly a magnificent athlete at six foot three and two hundred pounds. Donnie was quiet and brooding, seemingly malevolent, although one could never be exactly sure since he wasn't talking and we sure as hell weren't asking. In the beginning, I took his stoniness for ego, but in practice, he never asserted himself; in games, he was all but invisible; in fact, he didn't have much to be cocky about. Was it shyness? Maybe, but the night our game at U City digressed into a riot and both

116

benches emptied, we all witnessed a totally different and, for the moment, welcome side of Donnie Williams.

U City was mostly black and their team was on a terrible losing streak. In the second half of a close game, Bill recklessly raced for a loose ball, plunging headlong into the U City cheerleaders who were crouched courtside. What might have seemed like any player's fantasy instead became a mauling as they scratched, clawed, and pushed Bill around like he'd gone through a car wash with no car to protect him. Somebody jumped in to help before the Carnauba wax cycle and then both benches emptied. Once order was restored, we managed to win the game, exchanging pleasantries with the U City team before showering and heading into the winter night to our bus. And that's when we met up with the U City mob.

They stormed across the lot, throwing rocks and shouting, and we all made a beeline to our bus. We cowered inside, trying to confirm that we had everyone, and then pleaded with the driver to get going as rocks pelted the side and windows. The engine started, but when the mob began rocking the bus, our driver announced that we couldn't move until the rocking abated. We sat with our heads down, clinging to the seats in front of us like airplane passengers preparing for a crash, praying that nobody would pry open the door.

And then Donnie rose, silent and snorting, clad in a white fur coat, a manifestation of Shaft incarnate, and made his way to the front of the swaying bus. The driver popped open the door as Donnie leaned out from the bottom step. I don't know if he hollered or glowered, punched someone or just rose up and

117

expanded, but his physique and his countenance must have seemed imposing in the dim parking lot lights. None of us could see much as we peaked over our seats into the darkness. But that mob dissipated on the spot, and seconds later, we careened out of that lot toward safety. As we pulled ourselves up from the floor and into our seats, I glanced at Tice. "I know he broke up that crowd," I said, "but were they *running* from him?"

"No, not all of them," answered Tice. "Some of them were just sort of trotting."

But that was a one-time glimpse, never to be repeated again. Donnie's silence wasn't really menacing. His demeanor turned out to be indifference. He really had no interest in basketball, or school, or much of anything for that matter. A few years later, he would parlay an interest in and a talent for baseball, earning himself a minor league contract. But as far as I know, that's the only passion he ever showed.

We lost our last game heading into the Normandy Christmas Tournament, which we entered with a record of 3–3. Up and down. This time, I was the motivator at practice, acutely aware of the absence of comfort and joy when losing a first round game. I felt relieved when we won our first two tournament games to enter the semifinals, ensuring a practice-free holiday time. Our semifinal opponent would be Sumner High, denizens of the Public High League, all black, and seeded second. We'd not seen them play, although we had bumped into them in the locker room as they were leaving the floor and we were entering to play our second round game. They seemed big and strong and mean, an untamed herd to be feared and avoided. They brushed past, shoving us aside and bantering amongst themselves like a mob of sailors fresh off the ship.

Moulder and I wondered on occasion just how the Kirkwood blacks felt about the inner city blacks. Were the Public High players more soulful? Tougher? More athletic? Were suburban blacks intimidated? Were they somehow diluted by their association with whites? Did that make us whites an impurity to them? How would our black players respond to playing an all-black team, facing up to Sumner's blacks who stood shoulder to broad shoulder staring down on these honky-lovers?

Sumner crushed its first two opponents, including a fifty-point thrashing of Mehlville, a team we'd barely beaten by eight. Sumner was led by All Metro player Marshall Rogers, an incredibly strong and athletic six-foot-two guard who was quick enough to go around, strong enough to go through, and skilled enough to shoot over anyone. None of his physical gifts compared to the psychological warfare he waged, though, as he kept up a constant stream of trash talking, of a sort that was particularly demeaning in that he never spoke to you, but rather spoke about you to his teammates. He'd come off a pick to drain a shot and say, "That's right, brother, just pick his weak ass and I'll hit those all night." Then, exhorting his center to rebound, he'd say, "That punk can't stop you! Grab it and shove it back at him!" Finally, shouldering his way inside and then to the rim for a tough layup in traffic, he'd bark, "These muthafuckas ain't shit!"

And we weren't shit for the first quarter. It wasn't just our black players on their heels; it was all of us. While Rogers scored and ranted, Sumner's six-foot-seven-inch, 220 pound center, Ricky Brown, made the biggest impression on me. He'd shove me out of the way for rebounds and bump me out of where I wanted to go and what I wanted to do. We trailed by ten points at the end of the first quarter, and as we gathered between quarters, I glanced around our huddle and realized that it was all in my head. The thought that our blacks were scared or that Sumner was somehow empowered was all in my mind. We broke the huddle and Tommy, who never said anything, clapped his hands and muttered, "Let's go!" as much to himself as to the rest of us. And we proceeded to play them even the rest of the game. Rogers ended up with twenty-six points, but Tommy got eighteen off of him and played him even the last three quarters. I started pushing back on Ricky Brown and ended up with twenty-five points to his eighteen. Rogers led the tournament in scoring, but I was second, and as a group, we had passed a test, one that would pay off big time a year later.

Sumner won the Normandy Tournament, beating our archrival and previously unbeaten Webster Groves in the final, dominating Webster and winning by twenty. This gave us hope that our stronger showing against Sumner would bode well when we played Webster early in January. We took the floor at Webster armed with an array of full-court presses and buoyed by Bill's thirty point outburst in an overtime win against Parkway West four days earlier.

120

Our pressure defense had begun to wear on opponents, too, as Mr. Miller alternated between zone and man presses, never really overrunning opponents, but forcing them to protect the ball for long stretches that usually resulted in a few mistakes strung together, thereby fueling a Kirkwood run. Now that we were able to stay close to most teams, those runs made the difference. We'd just begun to practice Mr. Miller's Virginia zone press, a hybrid zone with man-to-man responsibilities, a terrific weapon for players as athletic as ours, but also a sophisticated design, demanding intimate knowledge and court awareness that we had yet to master. We had never before used it in a game.

We fell behind by six points early, and spent the rest of the game staying close and trying to catch up. Tommy went nuts from outside, canning jumper after jumper, but Webster's all-senior starting lineup was unfazed. We still trailed by six entering the fourth quarter. That's when we unveiled the Virginia zone press. Webster was confused. We were confused. I think the officials were confused, too, because when I drove the lane on a fast break, faked to a wing, and laid it in, I was whistled for a travel I didn't commit. When I looked at the official, he shrugged sheepishly and said softly, "I'm sorry." He wasn't the only one.

But a couple of late steals led to hoops, and when Tommy drained a free throw with forty-two seconds left, we had finally caught Webster, tied at seventy-three. Then Donnie Williams stole the inbound pass, so we worked for the last shot. Inside ten seconds, I looked down the lane as Donnie danced in and out, but I passed to Tommy figuring I'd feed the hot hand. Tommy slashed inside and hit a layup with two seconds left, but they whistled Donnie for three seconds. I knew they missed the call because Donnie had continued to dart in and out. The ref must have seen him in the lane, then looked away, and when he looked back, Donnie was in again. It was the same ref who'd called traveling earlier, so I gave him another stare that he ignored—no apology and no respite. Regardless, it was ball out to Webster on the sideline, game still tied, with two ticks left. Mr. Miller called time-out and put us in the Virginia zone press, probably figuring confusion would end the game one way or another, preventing overtime. Donnie was a sub, so I'm not sure how much practice he'd had with that particular zone; I know it was far less than the rest of us. He and I lined up in the backcourt closest to the Webster basket, and when both of our opponents streaked up court toward the inbounder and away from their basket, we followed. So when Webster forward Rich Race blew by us toward the Webster basket, we were flat-footed and hopelessly beaten.

As the inbound pass sailed over our heads, we had to choose: continue following our men up court or turn and give chase thus serving as poster children for Race's game winner. Donnie chose the former and I chose the latter, figuring the only thing worse than giving futile pursuit was letting him score all alone. Thus, it was I who showed up for a bird's-eye view of Race laying it in at the gun, and I who took the ball out of the net as the Webster fans rushed the floor. Our team ducked a shower of debris, bolting for the locker room while the fans in their euphoria swept up Race and me together for a triumphant march around the gym. My initial thought was that they were cheering his and my contributions to the Webster win and that mine had probably been greater than his given my flight up court freeing Race for that last look. It was a very brief ride for me, but in the few seconds it took for them to recognize and discard me, I crafted my post-game speech.

That hoop had been an accident since we really didn't know the Virginia zone that well; that's the only reason Race got by us so easily. And if Donnie had been there, he would've said the same thing. In fact, if Donnie had been there, he might've thrown on that Shaft coat of his and broken up that whole victory mob once and for all. But Donnie wasn't there then or any time after because the semester had just ended and he'd been ruled ineligible. That game marked the end of Donnie's tenure and the end of the Virginia zone press—forever. But despite our struggles with the Virginia press, the rest of our game was working, our pressure leading to turnovers, which led to run-outs, and eventually layups for our guards. Bill and Tommy combined for forty-seven of our seventy-three points that night, mostly off of forced turnovers.

We proceeded to roll through the second half of our conference season, sweeping every game except the Parkway West rematch. That was the game in which I'd chosen to try and pack the opposing center, fouling him to set up the winning free throws, and incurring Mr. Miller's wrath in the process. So minus my stupidity, we went undefeated the second half of conference play. Our rematch with Webster took place two

123

weeks later, this time on our floor. I was particularly motivated that night, not because Webster was our archrival, because I still didn't care much about those things. What got me going were Rich Race's wristbands. I had a good friend at church who was classmates with Race, and he told me that Race was bagging on my wristbands, these thin, pale red, threadbare bands that Harvey Love had given me when our football season ended. Love and I were standing in the locker room following a heartbreaking turkey day defeat to Webster (naturally), proclaiming Love's high school football career over, but vowing that the wristbands must live on, assigning their future to me. I wore them during the hoop season, mostly out of deference to Harvey with no particular attachment until Race decided to put a red Magic Marker to his own white bands, rendering them a splotchy pink and sporting them for our rematch. I thought it was pretty funny because my wristbands were pretty laughable, and I liked Race for putting me on. My favorite opponents were also those I most enjoyed challenging, so I went after Race and Webster with a vengeance.

The result was an overtime thriller with Kirkwood handing Webster its first and only league loss. The newspapers described a shootout between Webster's leading scorer, Sylvester Lofties, and me. Lofties went for twenty-two, but I topped him with twenty-six. Our win marked Kirkwood's first hoop win over Webster in three years. I knew nothing about the losing streak or any presumed duel with Lofties. To me, it was just another game like those at the Center or ones in the driveway. Off the dribble to the rim or pulling up for the jumper, it was a sequence of moves each setting up the next. I jerked Race all over that court, not because of a rivalry or a league championship, but because he beat me the previous time, dragging me into his postgame celebration in the process, and he rubbed my face in it just a little. I liked his style and I wanted to get him back—plain and simple.

We ended the regular season with a record of 15–10 having won six of our last eight games. We entered the regionals seeded fourth in an eight-team draw, meaning we would have to beat the five seed, the first seed, and the second seed to win it. Our top five players were underclassmen, and the newspapers and the opposing coaches were beginning to talk about us, not just for the following year, but possibly for that year too. We were tough to match up against. I was averaging nearly twenty a game, while Bill had scored thirty in one game, Tommy twenty-eight in another, and Jesse went for twenty-four in yet another. Our press was generating turnovers and fast break points, and we had emerged as a tough rebounding team with good size inside. I was now nearly six foot six and we brought six-eight Rhein Dabler and six-five Steve Schaper off the bench. Once again, the regionals were hosted by Webster, the top seed, so our challenge extended beyond the competition. I had crashed and burned there in two previous regionals, so history went against us as well.

We had exceeded any of our own expectations with a strong close to the regular season and so we had nothing to lose. In creating our pressure defense, Mr. Miller had not only leveraged our athleticism, he had made the game fun. We'd fly

125

all over the floor to the dismay and often the envy of other, more conservative teams, and more than one player shook my hand after a game, saying he wished he played in our system. We all felt a strong sense of pride in our team and in our coach, knowing that he was older and more experienced than other coaches with no limit to the depth of his knowledge. Plus, Mr. Miller knew every official by name—and that's what won our first round regional game.

Parkway West featured a pair of senior guards, Tom Webb and Jay Carey, who'd been touted as the strongest guards in the league. Our guards took exception to that. We came out swarming and prevented West from scoring a single first quarter field goal while opening up a six point lead. We pressed them and Webb and Carey kept dribbling it up, trading off scores with turnovers as we clung to a narrow lead. Early in the fourth quarter, trailing by only three, West turned up the pressure on us and forced Bill to pick up his dribble at midcourt. He pivoted a foot into the frontcourt and then back, and was whistled for a backcourt violation. I don't think he knew the rule, but he was determined not to let West pull it out of his hands. I didn't know the rule either, but Mr. Miller did. The rule states that a player is not in the frontcourt until both feet and the ball are in the frontcourt, so if a player puts a foot in and then pulls it out, he's not in violation.

The pressure of the moment—close game, noisy crowd—had both officials tensely pursing their lips. Had Mr. Miller accosted them, they would have held their ground and maybe even given him a technical. So Mr. Miller called time-out.

126

That gave him both time and room. I could hear him from our huddle as he approached the refs, calling their names and asking, "What did you see?" Under the circumstances, it was a brilliant question because it preempted any blustering or hiding behind the call. The ref said that he saw Bill's foot enter the frontcourt and then come out. "And?" asked Coach. That's all it took. The ref was forced to confess, "…and that's not a backcourt violation." Ball, momentum, and game to Kirkwood. Victory to Mr. Miller. Parkway West coach Mike Pratte was young, handsome, and a picture of sartorial splendor that night. Even so, he'd been undone by the red-faced old bald guy in the dated suit.

Two nights later, we faced Webster, the top seed, ranked fourth in the state, playing on their home floor, and the place was packed. We crowded together in the tiny visitor's locker room on the second floor, and Sam Weaver cast about for somewhere to spit out some phlegm. He finally chose an open window, stealing a glance as his spit bomb fell, and watching it nail some hoodlum below. Sam was black and the hoodlum was black, but a very different looking black. As the guy hollered up at him, Sam gave a nervous apology and pulled back from the window. I had to take a look and I couldn't believe how many people had swarmed the building. Judging from the crowd noise already reverberating from inside, I wondered where all those other folks would go. As it turned out, they hung around outside after being turned away due to a packed house, eventually duking it out, Kirkwood thugs versus Webster thugs, while we fought like dogs inside for the duration of the game.

127

But in hindsight, Webster never had a chance, not with Race insisting on sporting those damn Magic Marker pink wristbands. I'd told Harvey about the insult to the wristbands, jokingly suggesting that he'd been implicated along with me. Sure enough, when we took the floor, Harvey was glaring at Race from the stands. He hollered at me, "Kill that muthafucka and his wristbands!" And I did—again. We hit them with a monster second quarter, grabbed the lead, and held it despite a spirited late rally, and this time I was getting the postgame tour of the gym on Kirkwood fans' shoulders after dropping twenty-six on them and sealing a four point victory.

I had exorcised two demons: beating Webster on its home floor and advancing to the regional final. We faced second seed Vianney on a Friday night playing against the athletic Charlie Shell and the sharpshooting guard, Tom Rothschild. I loved watching Rothschild. He'd launch a bomb, and when it splashed the net, he'd hold his pose, arm extended, wrist pronated, admiring his work, and then turn back down court still extending that arm, like a warship's cannon cocked and ready to fire. One of our guys asked him prior to the tip how he was doing. "My guns are oiled and ready." I loved that. He lit us up for twenty-two that night, but his was not the fastest gun in the game. Bill's was.

Mr. Miller brought Bill off the bench all season, an energy boost that never failed to ignite a Kirkwood run. When Bill hit the floor that night, he seemed shot from a cannon, tearing through Vianney for layups, jumpers, and free throws. In the second half, during which neither team led by more than

128

four, Bill went nine for twelve from the field, driving Vianney Coach Jerry Boeckman to distraction. Per the next morning's paper, Boeckman vowed to find out what parish Moulder lived in, perhaps hoping to recruit him to Catholic school Vianney.

Fourth quarter, tie game, a minute to go. Rothschild had just hit a jumper and pulled down his gun as we set up on offense. Tommy fed Billy in the deep corner and I darted to the near block, sealing Charlie and now wide open for an entry pass. Bill looked me in the eye and I already knew that I'd turn high and pump fake Charlie into the rafters and then spin back for an easy layup, scoring so quickly that I'd be able to run past Charlie while he was still hanging there, and give him the what-the-hell-were-you-possibly-thinking-and-why-are-you-still-up-there look, chiding him that we weren't at the Center and Ricky Nelson was nowhere in sight. And oh yeah, you lose.

Bill raised the ball, glanced my way one more time, and shot. I knew he was hot, but he was just a sophomore. I thought I was the man. I was older, more experienced, and that possession was for all the marbles. As Bill released it, I started to turn inside for a rebound, but I saw the look in his eye: "It's in." Not "it has a chance" or "it felt good out of my hand." "It's in". Furthermore "I knew it was in before I shot it, and at that moment in time, given a choice between feeding you for a spin against Charlie or hoisting up this twenty footer out here, at that moment, mine was a better shot than yours."

Splash. Bucket. Game. Thirty-one for the Thrill, a sophomore, off the bench, in Vianney's face. That's all that mattered: beating Charlie Shell and gaining bragging rights at

129

the Center the next morning, grounding Rothschild's air attack (though I began practicing his arm and wrist pose in the shower later, considering adopting the move, but figuring it had no place in our pressure *D*, and it would probably land me on the bench plus it was irritating my fellow bathers). We had won the regional, earning a spot in the state tournament Sweet Sixteen. In the bus we huddled up, not to cheer our victory or revel in our success, but to plan our Saturday morning. "You going to the Center tomorrow?" "Hell yeah." "You think Charlie's gonna show?" "He'd better. Else I'll have to go to his house and bring his sorry ass down there." Charlie did show, proud and defiant, answering every taunt with his own smack. He played his ass off too.

#22, Bill "The Thrill" Moulder

Chapter 7

It's half time. Just like that, the horn sounds and I'd say everybody stopped, but that would suggest that everyone was moving in the first place, which would be false. Billy buried those two free throws, but from then on...I can't really remember. The scoreboard reads 21–20, Raytown. They scored six straight? We only scored twenty for the entire half? That's barely a quarter's worth of points for us.

There's a short stairway and both teams crowd together as we head for the locker rooms. We're shoulder to shoulder, all mixed in, and I take a deep breath, and proclaim in a voice directed at Raytown, but loud enough that both teams can hear, "Fellas, that score is an embarrassment to both teams. Let's turn it up a little in the second half, OK?" A couple of Raytown players look at me bewildered, but Geppetto's right there chiming in. "The score's just fine, Rogers, fine right where it is." Shut up! I almost had them. No, I didn't. They're robots, programmed. I can't get inside their metal casings.

There's nothing to say at half time. Our defense is good, we just need to get a few turnovers and convert them into run-outs. I have no idea what a horrid field goal percentage and free throw percentage we're shooting. Mr. Miller knows, he's holding a stat sheet, but he doesn't say. It wouldn't change things anyway. You either make them or you don't. I glance around the room at the bowed heads of the starters, sitting and picking at their fingers and at the substitutes standing around. They're usually chatting and rustling, feeding off the game and stirring things up, getting ready for some second-half minutes behind a big lead, but right now, they're shifting from foot to foot, chewing their lips like cows in a field. We might as well get back out there and warm up, and try to start making shots. We rise and move through the door, back onto the court where our crowd greets us, enthused, but also tentative. Raytown's crowd cranes their necks awaiting their heroes.

A quick layup line and then we shoot, balls banging the rim and backboard, going up faster and more desperately. Raytown takes the floor accompanied by a roar, looking smooth and assured. I think, "What are you so jazzed about? Twenty-one points in a half and you're strutting?" And I meant it; it's embarrassing. At least we're chagrined. Raytown's guys are clueless. I glance again at the scoreboard, 21–20 in Raytown's favor, and then I survey my guys, trying to summon some energy, bouncing around and swinging their arms like cold commuters at a bus stop trying to stay warm. It's the only time all season we've trailed at the half.

It's not like we've never played a close game, just not this year. The closest any team came during the regular season was fourteen points. The closest in the tournament was nine except for Northwest but those guys were legit. Last season, every game was close and we thrived on that. I scan my fellow starters figuring I'll get mine this half. We just need somebody else to make a shot or two, and that will ignite the whole inferno. A couple of steals, a couple layups, and we'll run over them. They appear to have too little firepower to come from behind. Get them down six or eight, and they'll roll over. Teams always

133

do. Dabler will start the half in place of Jesse making us six-foot-eight, six-foot-six, and six-foot-four across the front line. The game's already slow, so that shouldn't hurt. Meanwhile, we should dominate the boards.

Center jump to start the quarter and we've switched baskets, so now when the ref tosses it off center, it's directly over my head and not Stolle's. A tip to Billy, two dribbles, and a pass ahead to Rock, but 33 just tips it away preventing a layup. I holler over to the bench for an inbounds play, and they call my number. Rock enters to me for a five-foot banker and we're up one. Stolle makes a free throw to tie it and Billy comes right back with an eighteen-footer. That's what I'm talking about. One or two more of those and it will open everything up inside.

They nail a corner jumper to tie it again. This is fun. Tommy looks inside to Dabler and their whole zone collapses on him, so when I show at the near elbow, I'm open for Tommy's lob. I catch and shoot in one motion, and again, Stolle's late. Even if I had missed, Rock and Dabler were inside for the rebound. But I'm not missing, not right now in my own driveway with the spotlights shining down among the leaves in the darkness. My dad's in a lawn chair sipping evening coffee, while my mom washes dishes, and I talk a constant flow of trash at Mitch. Every make gives us a chance to press. We're pressing man-to-man and falling back into a 2–3 zone with Rock in the middle. We coax a miss and Billy pulls up on the break. He hits me trailing at the free throw line. One dribble around Stolle and lay it in. We're up four and that roar is our crowd, drowning out Raytown and putting the hop back in our step. Tommy slaps his hands and steps past me to press up, smacks Dabler on the butt, and jumps his man.

134

Tommy's funny. Not funny ha ha, but funny peculiar. He doesn't cuss. When he's really pissed or frustrated, he'll grit his teeth and bark, "Goodness!" He says it heavy on the G, so you think maybe it's going to be "God!" or "God dammit!" When he's really pumped up, he'll clap his hands once or twice, but that's it. That Dabler butt slap is the most animated I think I've ever seen him. I've wondered this season if there's been some times when he wanted more shots, more points. No doubt if he were playing on any other team he'd average twenty a game easy. None of that now, though. He's just pulling on his share of the rope; we all are. And finally, it's starting to move.

Rock

Day after day
Alone on a hill
The man with the foolish grin is keeping perfectly still
—"The Fool on the Hill," The Beatles

To a black person, racism and prejudice must have been like a dull ache. One morning, you wake up and suddenly sense its presence. At the same time, you realize that it's been there longer than just this morning, though you can't recall exactly when it started, but it's been there as long as you can remember, and now that you notice, the pain has begun to intensify. As you explore a little and talk about it, you learn that others have the same pain. Theirs dates back to before they can remember and someone says that it's because of those white folks. And so you

135

start to scrutinize white folks, certain attitudes and actions expressed by a few of them—things you never would have noticed before. Those acts suddenly assume new meaning; they're malicious and deceitful. Other whites, though not quite as hurtful, nevertheless reflect indifference to and tolerance for those other acts, and that attitude renders its bearers as guilty as the racists. And once you recognize the pain, you search for its cause, only to find that it's so pervasive, it's been there for so long, that you can't eradicate it no matter how hard you try. There is no vaccine and no cure. Worse yet, it is woven into the very fabric of your life. It is society itself that harbors this pain and feeds it. You brace yourself and vow to overcome the pain through stoicism and character. Still, the pain is relentless and just as persistent as you promised yourself you would be. Eventually, anger and frustration set in, and you fight it, you hit back, you rail against it, but you're no more than an infant writhing against an adult, so even as you twist and pull, halfway out of your jacket, you sense that this thing has you by the sleeve, and all you are doing is spending yourself. You are left with the pain. Everyone has endured pain, but most times, they do so knowing that eventually the pain will subside. But not this pain and not you. After all of your discovery and rationalization and fortitude and protests, after all of that you look around at your fellow sufferers and at those more fortunate, some of whom empathize and some of whom twist the knife (and you can't tell them apart, so eventually you dislike or distrust them all), and you are forced to accept the one eventuality you swore you would never abide: there is nothing you can do.

136

Gloria Louise Williams knew something about the pain. She had long since stopped looking for the cure or even a pain reliever, and instead, she had placed her faith in understanding—understanding the pain, understanding its victims, and understanding its inflictors. It hadn't taken her long to realize that it was a white man's world and living successfully within that world depended on assimilation. Not capitulation and not confirmation of injustice and prejudice, but optimization of one's self and one's position in that world. So she raised her children to integrate with white people, to learn to live with them, and to draw knowledge from and even some control over them while maintaining one's station and pride. She preached self-confidence and self-sufficiency through involvement versus isolation. "Learn from the white man," she counseled her brood. "You don't have to become him, but you sure as hell better understand him." She raised seven girls and four boys on that credo, and it was the youngest boy who mastered it, used it, and ultimately brandished it to an extent beyond anything she had envisioned or hoped for.

Robert Williams never knew his father. He thought he knew his three older brothers. They'd been his first and only friends and the architects of the makeshift hoop nailed to a tree in the backyard of their house. The four of them would play there all day and well into the night, frolicking and laughing, pushing and shoving. He thought he knew them and he thought they knew him until the day oldest brother Sam loaded up his brothers in his car and headed out to a game. Robert chased after them only to hear that there wasn't enough room for him in the car, in the game, at all. He stood crying for them to come back for him and for the game. But they didn't come back. They continued to drive back and forth to games without Robert. They left him alone and fatherless again.

Robert's mom moved the whole brood to north Kirkwood and told each of them to find their way in the world, defend themselves, and fight back. Valley Park had hardened him; whites called him nigger and the few whites that did befriend him were labeled nigger-lovers. It was a nightmare. Following his mother's counsel, Robert steeled himself, balling his fists and vowing to never back down, never let them make him cry again. He became a rock. His first day in Kirkwood, Rock went walking through town, looking around for nothing in particular, but determined to find his way and carve out his space. Maybe it was a father figure he sought, but what he found was a game. Locker Room Smith, bouncing a basketball in the family driveway spotted a tall, black kid standing in the street, pretending not to stare and feigning indifference, ignoring Locker Room's call until he approached and Rock could see the kid's intent. In a strange neighborhood surrounded by whites, adrift and alone, the game hooked him and reeled him in. By the time they finished playing that first day, Mr. Smith was watching them, and as the quiet black kid walked off down his driveway, the dad hollered after that he was welcome to come back any time to shoot, even if Locker Room wasn't home. Rock grinned at that, the fact that any white family would trust a black kid to come around their house any time, some black kid they didn't know and who hated white people, neighbors liable to stare out their windows and eventually chastise the Smiths as nigger-lovers. Stupid.

But Rock returned regularly and soon became a fixture in the Smith driveway, schooling Locker Room in street moves, while Locker room taught him to raise his release point from his hip to his forehead. All the while, Mr. Smith watched from the porch, filling a void in Rock that the boy never knew he had. To Rock's surprise, scores of Kirkwood whites accepted him without scorn, and at school he adopted a quiet, background presence away from confrontation.

It was the summer of 1970 and Rock befriended a couple of white hoop players, Scott Schulte and Dick Russell. The three of them roamed the South County looking for games. One day, they came up against Jesse, Tommy, and Jesse's brother, Willie, on a playground court. Rock was new to Kirkwood and didn't know these three blacks, had no idea that two of them would become friends and teammates. All he knew was that the game was close, contested, and contentious to the point that tempers flared and fists closed. Schulte and Russell were intimidated, but not Rock. Black or white, it made no difference. He wasn't backing down. He got in all of their faces, swearing he'd whup any of them, and if he couldn't whup them all, he'd go get his brothers and together they would.

That fall, Rock entered KHS as a sophomore, ineligible for hoop the first semester, but practicing with the team as his older brother Donnie played, parading his white fur coat, and eventually lost his eligibility at the semester just as Rock gained his. So Rock inherited Donnie's uniform, number 42, and the newspapers continued to report his results as Donnie Williams, an inconspicuous debut and a hint of things to come. Rock avoided publicity and attention, almost to a fault. In practice he was brilliant, a six-foot-four gazelle who glided effortlessly up court with a great handle, smooth moves, and a sweet midrange jump shot. Years of street ball preceded by backyard thrashings at the hands of his three older brothers had forged a soft touch and hard resolve. He had never played organized ball and thus was devoid of the single biggest governor of on-court behavior and doubt: a conscience.

Rock played the fool, shifting between a brooding silence and nonsensical streams of consciousness, adopting no social circle, independent of blacks and whites, and choosing his friends from among various groups without regard for color or station. No one really understood him and no one ever got too close. One day he'd ignore you and the next, he'd be joking and laughing, extending his hand and saying solemnly, "Hey, we OK, ain't we?" to which most would extend their hand in agreement, only to be met with, "No we ain't!" as he'd yank his hand back and stare before breaking into uncontrollable laughter, hands clapping at his own joke. Keeping everything at arm's length, Rock would have been a psychologist's dream if only he could be coaxed to the couch, a diagnosis of insecurity, lack of self-confidence, or "in search of a father figure" sure to arise. I always felt like he was smarter than all that, the array of characters he adopted merely a veil behind which he could play, Peter Pan in shorts, never growing up, and always performing but never in the starring role.

140

That was a big part of Rock. He was probably the most athletic and gifted of all of us, but he lacked the interest or desire to lead or even shine. He was mostly guarded, cloaking his incredible talent with a somber on-court mien, only occasionally responding to the irresistible allure of the game when he would run off three or four spectacular scores or steals, jaw-dropping displays of brilliance that won games by coincidence. Rock focused on destroying an opposing player or silencing a crowd, a game within the game within the game, challenges so tiny and insignificant that they were invisible to any but him. These glimpses resulted in high anticipation devoid of expectation, rendering all of us like parents who one day discover their kid cleaned his room and then tiptoe around in hopes of a trend, but never mention it for fear that identification will cause eradication. Rock was like door number one on the TV show *Let's Make a Deal*. The audience has seen the booby prize so often that they come to expect it, but deep inside they harbor just a little hope because of that one time when it opened to the trip to Hawaii.

Once he became eligible, Rock became a factor, albeit an unpredictable one. Most games, he'd come off the bench, grab a couple of rebounds, make a shot or two, and log eight or ten nondescript minutes in the shadows of Donnie's name and number in the box score. But our run through the regionals resonated with him as it did with all of us, the tug of the game threading its way inside him and drawing him out of his shell and into our team. He didn't score much in those regional games, but he showed that he could rebound and defend, and in

141

so doing, he relaxed a little, opening up and joining in the bus ride banter. He was the one carrying on about Charlie Shell after the regional final, followed by a merciless rant of smack the next day at the Center. For Rock, it hadn't been about beating Vianney or winning the regional. It was about kicking Charlie's butt; more importantly, it was about bragging rights at the next day's games, leverage that Rock craved madly and wielded brazenly, the game within the game.

Our next tournament game was scheduled for the following Monday night, March 8, 1971, a historic date in sports, the night that Muhammad Ali met Joe Frazier at Madison Square Garden in New York to contest the Fight of the Century. I wanted to listen to the fight on the radio, having followed Ali's return from exile through a couple of tune-up bouts preparing him for this championship fight, but our game was scheduled at the exact same time as the fight. I would have to read about it the next day.

The fight represented a rare matchup between two undefeated heavyweights, each a champion. Going in, Frazier owned the championship, which had been stripped of Ali when he refused induction into the Army. Frazier was 26–0 with twenty-three knockouts and Ali was 31–0 with twenty-five knockouts. Both were blacks who had overcome childhood poverty and a lack of education to rise to the pinnacle of their profession. Each had won an Olympic gold medal, Ali in 1960 as a light heavyweight and Frazier the heavyweight gold in 1964. They were each guaranteed $2.5 million for the fight, a record purse at that time.

142

But despite all that they had in common, society was determined to split them apart. In the absence of a white contender, Frazier was cast as the white man's champion, mostly because he opposed a Black Muslim who had befriended Malcolm X, turned his back on his country's call to military duty, and embraced the civil rights movement. The media placed Frazier on a pedestal, predicting victory while minimizing the chances of Ali, the upstart. They did the same thing to Kirkwood leading up to our game that night.

Our opponent, Bayless High, emerged from its regional with a 23–2 record and a ten-game winning streak. All white, they were a senior-heavy team that had gone deep in the state tournament the previous year. Kirkwood, now starting three blacks, was labeled a dark horse with our eleven losses and a young team. Denver Miller thought so little of our regional chances that he bought a bus ticket to Columbia to attend a basketball reunion the night of our game, a trip he happily forwent, but an indication of the odds against us. In everyone's minds, Bayless was Frazier and we were Ali. And I liked that—a lot.

Between Friday night's regional final and Monday night's game, we had no opportunity to practice, just a couple of hours of Saturday hoop and jive at the Center. Mr. Miller had time to review his game scoring system, though, and realized that Bill Moulder had earned the start, a dilemma for our coach because he preferred Bill's energy off the bench. But he stuck to his system and so that night, for the first time all year, he started all underclassmen: juniors Tommy, Jesse, and me, along with sophomores Rock and Bill.

This was our best pressure lineup by far and by now we were imposing it on everyone we played. No guard could dribble through it and no team was prepared to pass around it, at least not sustainably. We had yet to develop prowess, but what we had by then was an identity. And we were loose. Despite the papers minimizing us, we were confident in our game plan and in our players. I stepped into the center circle for the opening tip just as Ali stepped forward for round one.

We both got off to fast starts, Kirkwood pestering Bayless all over the floor as Ali stuck and moved against Frazier, peppering him with jabs and raising welts across his face, winning the first three rounds. But in the fourth round, Frazier caught up, catching Ali with several thunderous hooks and pinning him against the ropes. That's also when Jeff Zehner went to work for Bayless. Through the first five minutes of the game, Bayless tried to pass against our press, but to no avail. We prevented them from getting the ball to their leader, Jim Prueshner, a six-foot-four, 230 pound slugger. So they began throwing it in to Zehner, clearing out to let him dribble. Nobody had dribbled through our press that year, but Zehner did, over and over again. Working at the back of the press, I had a great view of Zehner darting up court, like a high-performance sports car weaving in and out of orange cones. Zehner left Tommy and Bill and Jesse in his wake, streaking toward me, then he'd pull up on a dime to dish to a cutter or drop a short jumper. And once into the frontcourt, Bayless got it to Prueshner, who punished us by scoring, rebounding, and pushing us around like wimps at the beach.

We bent, but we didn't break, pulling together and working our way back into the game, unable to create turnovers off the press, but challenging Zehner and doubling down on Prueshner. We scored to end the third quarter and trailed by only two while Ali fought on against Frazier, surviving a vicious hook in the eleventh round, and entering the fifteenth and final round behind but in contention. We gathered around Mr. Miller before the final period and he didn't have to say a thing. We had this. Bill and Tommy talked animatedly about trapping Zehner, while Jesse offered to put a body on Prueshner, and I vowed to handle six-foot-eight Jim Baker myself. Rock stared into the distance and shook his head. "If he shoulders in there one more time, I'm gonna whup his ass," he said softly. Who? "That big dude. Just see if I don't." Classic Rock. No score, no circumstance, just his own game within the game. A great way to block out distractions, though.

Fourth quarter was a classic, with both teams up and down the floor, Bayless stretching its lead to seven, and us fighting back to within three. Rock threw everything he had at Prueshner, who outweighed him by at least forty pounds, and I got the hot hand, scoring eleven in the period to finish with twenty-six including twelve of thirteen from the free throw line. I generally shot less than 70 percent from the line, preferring pickup games at the Center to practicing free throws. But that night, I got into a zone, especially in the fourth quarter. Bayless would score, we'd come down, and it seemed as though every time I caught it, they'd foul me. My first free throw of the night, I put it up soft and it bumped the rim a little then settled in, and although I lacked the kind of stroke to swish them all, I realized that I could duplicate what I'd just done. By the time I got to the fourth quarter, I was throwing darts, seven of seven down the stretch, each shot keeping us close, and none of them a challenge as I just kept easing them inside the rim, *bumpa, bumpa,* and in.

In the final two minutes of our game as well as the final round of the fight, both of us faltered, Frazier flooring Ali with a fifteenth round hook even as Bayless ripped through our press one more time to gain a seven point lead to end it. The favored contestants won and the media had their darlings. But we were undaunted and so was Ali. He would go on to a string of victories, eventually regaining the championship and avenging his loss to Frazier. And our team would do the same. Our starting lineup would remain intact for the following year, stronger for having played and lost to Bayless. It was the last time anyone would dribble through our press and the last time we would ever face a better team.

#10, Showtime Grice, passing to Rock, #42

Chapter 8

I think we're under their skin a little. After my layup, they inbound and push it up the left side, and 40 rushes a corner jumper that's short. I rebound and turn outside, and I'm passing to a spot without even looking because I know Billy's there; we've practiced our break over and over and over. He dribbles hard up the sideline and they're back, but we've practiced that, too. He slows his dribble and gets to the top of the key—secondary break, see who shows. It's Dabler, running that big body hard, and he gets to the left block, where he's been taught to run, and when he looks back to Billy, the ball is already there. He plants his feet, dribbles once into the lane, and shoots a skyhook. Rock and I both have inside rebounding position, but forget it. Rhein's fully extended and he's shooting down at the basket, and it's like dropping a tennis ball into a well. It's 30–24, Kirkwood, time-out Raytown, and our crowd is going berserk. I glance at Geppetto on my way to the huddle and he's staring holes through his guys like laser beams. This is not the pace they want. It took a little longer than last night, but that's OK. Raytown's better than Carthage was. But the lead is six with five and a half minutes left in the third. The momentum has swung.

I've sized them up. They can't be a good come-from-behind team. They're too slow and they can't push the tempo. If they do, they'll play right into our hands. We love it helter-skelter. The only team that tried to run with us this year was U City at their place. Devoid of Donnie Williams and his Shaft coat, I suppose they were feeling bold. The ball never stopped moving that night and we dropped 108 on them, a three and a half points-per-minute pace as we beat them by thirty-one. I allow myself to think about that for a moment. Maybe my halftime guilt trip got through to them and they'll step on the gas.

Raytown inbounds against our press and we're amped. Billy and Tommy trap 22 in the backcourt and he hurls it up the sideline, which is exactly what we want. I've hedged, and although 30 is there, I've got time to cut in front. Because 22 is alone upcourt, all I have to do is bat it back and we'll have a two-on-one, and that's money. It'll be our bucket, an eight point lead, and all the momentum. The ball is tailing out of bounds, so I plant both feet and lean over the sideline just in front of Raytown's cheerleaders...hmmm, they've got nice, new uniforms, too, just like their team. Our cheerleaders wear these red wool sweaters and they must sweat like mad inside those things, especially now that it's spring, and today was like sixty-five degrees. Stretching out for the ball is no sweat, just like in football, keeping both feet inbounds, plus nobody's gonna crush me...unless I clear the raised floor and crash into the press row, but I don't care because I'll just jump back up, and maybe now's the time to race over there and put a finger in Geppetto's face.

*Lay out, catch, and toss it into the backcourt. My momentum carries me within a foot of the radio guys and I can hear one announcing, "...and Rogers steals that one, but Raytown's got it." What? Sure enough, 22 kept coming and grabs the ball, flips it ahead to 52 in the far corner; he takes a jab step at Dabler to create space, and then launches a twenty footer—*swish! *You mustn't let that guy shoot.*

Anybody else, but not him. So the lead's not eight, it's four, and next time down 52 gets the same look and buries another. We miss and 22 comes down, puts a spin move on Tommy, and nails a fifteen-foot turnaround, and it's tied. Damn! We call time-out and Mr. Miller's drawing something up, but I'm staring across at where I got that steal. We had them...

A few minutes later, it's still tied, I get a rebound, and I'm gonna fire it ahead because Billy said he'd leak out. He's at the far free throw line, and just as I let it go, I see 22 streaking back, so I put a lot on it and Billy leaps to get it as 22 just misses. Billy feeds Tommy for a layup and that's points in transition, baby, and a two-point lead. They get it to 40 on my side and he gives me that jab step, but I know what's next and I pack him clean, grab it, and outlet to Billy. His pass to Tommy is deflected, but Tommy knocks it to Rock right under the hoop, and his little banker rolls out, but Rhein bats it against the backboard as everybody jumps, and when it bounces back out, they all have to come down except for Rhein, who doesn't jump much so he's standing there, six-foot-eight with his hands up high, and calmly banks it home, and we're up four.

It's late in the quarter now and we get a steal, kick it ahead to me, and I'm dribbling in on 52 who slides over to take away my right hand. I bring it behind my back and step across into the key, but my dribble hits the back of my foot and I lose it. The quarter ends in a tie and I shake my head. Number 52 says something and Geppetto's clapping his hands like mine was a stupid move, going behind my back when I'm a center and not a guard, but hell, I always make that move. I had 52 beat and sure, I turned it over, but that's how I play, I'm going to attack you, beat you, and maybe toss you a look as I run back. I'm sure as hell not going to pull it out and wait for reinforcements when you're all I've got to beat. Pickup game or state final, it doesn't matter.

The Calm

> There you stood on the edge of your feather
> Expecting to fly
> —"Expecting to Fly," Neil Young

Two nights later, four of us piled into my car—Bill, Tommy, Jesse, and me—to follow Bayless down to Kiel Auditorium for their quarterfinal game, which seemed perfectly natural at the time. We figured that if they kept winning, it meant that we were that much closer to parity with the remaining teams in the state tournament. Engaged in idle chatter until I got to Highway 40, I then began to speed and weave around cars, until suddenly it got stone quiet in the back seat, and I glanced in the mirror to see Tommy's eyes widen like he's seen a ghost. Jesse stared out the window, pushing away from the door like maybe it was going to tear right off. I thought, "This is how I always drive," and Tommy's lips moved, but nothing came out. Finally, Tommy blurted out, "Fire up some music," and when I did, my 8-track stereo played Cat Stevens, which broke the spell as Tommy winced and looked at Jesse and asked, "Who's that old buzzard?" It was phrased as a question begging not to be answered, so I rifled through the other tapes, and found Neil Young, James Taylor, just a couple more

151

buzzards, plus Black Sabbath, and I didn't even want to think how that would fly, so I flipped on the radio thinking that my pop station might be playing some Motown. Instead, the Carpenters were playing, so I flicked it off. We were nearly there anyway.

We walked inside Kiel, an aging downtown arena that once housed the St. Louis Hawks before they flew off to Atlanta. My dad had taken me there once to see Cliff Hagan, Lenny Wilkens, and Jumping Joe Caldwell play the Detroit Pistons, and as we entered the arena, I wondered why my dad ever did that at a time when I didn't play hoops and he'd never been to a game. We sat in the old push-down arena seats, like a movie theater only unpadded, sipping on overpriced, watered-down Cokes, and watched Bayless lose a close one to DeSoto, and it was unanimous: we would have pressed DeSoto out of the gym. Vashon took the floor and annihilated DeSmet, and we realized that we were no match for them. We rose to leave and noticed that it was a Public High League crowd, all black and boisterous, and Bill mentioned something about Vashon's star, Roscoe Simmons, like, "Roscoe's got some game," and two guys stopped him saying, "You know Roscoe?" and Bill was like, "Well, I don't *know* Roscoe except for watching him," and the two guys dismissed us, so we moved more quickly for the exits. I glanced back once more and the thought crossed my mind, just for a fleeting moment, "That will be us down there next year," not as a vow or a goal or any inspiration, but more like, "That would be cool," but it wasn't real. It was spring, time for baseball and girls. The next season was light years away.

We were just faces in a crowd that night, watching other teams make headlines and history, ignored but for our brief encounter with the Roscoe Fan Club. We had nothing in common with each other except for our defeat by Bayless, and although I neither knew nor cared at the time, it was the only instance where the four of us would go anywhere or do anything together except to practice and play hoop. After that, we dispersed. Bill, Tommy, Rock, and Jesse all played varsity baseball in the spring. I had played varsity baseball the previous spring, but opted out of the following season for two reasons: one being the monotony of year-round sports, and the other being Scott Markle.

I was a shortstop. Despite my height, I had good range and good hands, and I had played the position repeatedly. I was moved to first base my sophomore year in deference to senior shortstop Jim Hughes, and was headed back to shortstop the next year. But the summer before my junior year, I was playing boundary ball (a version of over-the-line) at Meramec JC when this kid stepped up and hit the first pitch over the fence, over the far parking lot, and out of sight. He was an averaged sized guy, maybe five-foot-ten, weighing a buck fifty, but as sweet a swing as I'd ever seen. I complimented him on his blast and he smiled self-consciously, said he was going to be a sophomore at KHS and he played shortstop. "OK, so I can retire this year," I thought, 'leaving not so much as a cleat mark out at short, because this kid is going to handle that spot for the next three years, leading the team in all sorts of categories without so much as a 'What ever happened to Drew?'"

The summer of 1971 was a study in contrasting approaches to high school basketball. Northwest High School in the Public High League had nearly beaten state champ Vashon and returned most of its starters, all of whom spent the summer playing pick-up ball at various tough venues in downtown St. Louis. They played against older, stronger players and refined their skills for hours on end, day after day, in sweltering heat on paved courts with no nets and no mercy. They shoved and fought, shooting and practicing, honing skills in preparation for a run through the toughest, most competitive high school league in the state of Missouri. This regimen continued through the fall, as none of them played football, thereby freeing them up to concentrate on hoop alone.

Raytown South was a basketball program ahead of its time. State champions in 1970 and contenders in 1971, they sported three incoming starters who had rostered for that 1970 championship, sitting on the bench and practicing through the entire run, learning firsthand what it took and how to prepare. Coach Geppetto opened the school gym on summer evenings, overseeing shoot-arounds, skill drills, and scrimmages, abiding the rule that prohibits actual coaching while strongly encouraging players to work on this or that. His center, Ed Stolle, diligently ran stairs in ankle weights to generate the hops that would win them all four regulation jump balls, plus the overtime jump in their quarterfinal win against a very athletic Kansas City Central team. They fostered and taught teamwork, rehearsing solutions to every conceivable barrier including full-court zone presses of the sort that Kirkwood eventually threw at them.

And then there was Kirkwood High. With no open gym time because Mr. Miller was not authorized to do so, each of us sweating our way through our own summers, occasionally crossing paths at the Center, but mostly remaining on our own, four of us playing on different summer baseball teams, acknowledging each other but little more. During one night game, I attempted to move Rock off the plate with a sidearm fastball, which he deposited over the road in left field, a feat that rendered him so tickled he could barely circle the bases, laughing and clapping his hands, crossing home plate, and stopping en route to the dugout as I rubbed up a new one, and hollered, "We still alright, ain't we?" I started to nod, and before I could stop myself, it was too late, as he was already crying out, "No, we ain't," a jab he found so hilarious that he required assistance to negotiate the remaining walk to the dugout.

Mr. Miller encouraged participation in other sports, I suppose figuring that if he couldn't formally practice us, then we better play other sports versus hanging out, getting into trouble. That's exactly where I was headed the night I emerged from a car full of beer-drinking, underage friends to head into a party. At once, I saw Rock and we chatted just in time for the cops to pull up and bathe us in spotlight. They were all over two kids puking next to the car, plus two more carrying six-packs of beer. When they got to us, one held his flashlight over his head, pointing it into my eyes, and I squinted like Dracula emerging from a cave, and I was already rehearsing what I would tell my father, still hoping to talk my way out of the predicament. Just like that, the cop stopped and pulled down his flashlight.

"Hello, Robert."

"Hey, officer."

"What are you doing here?"

"We was going into this party."

"You drinking?"

"No, sir."

And the next thing I knew, we were standing in a darkened yard, no cops, no lights, and no hassle.

"Rock," I asked him, "how do you know that cop?"

"I don't know him, but I guess he knows me."

"But how?"

"I think from the night my brothers and me got into it at a Dairy Queen. He was one of the cops that came."

"But you don't know for sure."

"Nope."

So much for our summer of preparation.

My summer jobs were sealing driveways (pushing black tar around asphalt in ninety-five degree heat) and umpiring baseball games in the bayou at Marshall Field, my blue umpire uniform the canvas for various, melted, snow cone creations wrought by the humidity. I often joined the daily boundary ball games at the high school, lob-and-hit affairs positioned so that only the most majestic of drives cleared the fence to the football field. Each player chose his own pitcher, who would serve up meatballs as in batting practice, enabling monster drives on every swing, games moving smartly along except when one guy (who shall remain nameless lest he perceive a criticism in a simple recount of his pickiness) would step up, choose his pitcher, and proceed to take dozens of pitches looking for just the right one while we languished in the field, crossing our arms, and shifting from one foot to the other. The sweltering heat extracted every ounce of moisture through our skin, depositing it onto our shirtless backs, throats parched, and vultures beginning to circle until we hollered at him to please, just take a hack. He'd watch indignantly as another toss failed to find his precise spot, finally staring accusingly out at his hand-picked lackey like the guy was pitching around him.

We were still playing plenty of hoop. Several times a week, a bunch of us gathered at Bad Dude Carnahan's house for some of that "driveway shit" Cecil used to chide me about. The court was cramped and concrete, and the games were bloodbaths, particularly when Jim Moulder played, locking into tense battles with younger brother Bill, who was now old enough to hold his own. They went at it like savages, none of us aware of their history and the revenge that Bill sought, or the subsequent ice baths and agony that an aging Jim suffered rather than concede anything to his brother.

Rock, meanwhile, had taken to heading downtown on summer evenings, cruising for pickup games in a car full of buddies, oftentimes opposing Public High League players, taunted and threatened, but never giving an inch. He answered trash talk about city blacks' superiority to county blacks with his own smack, finding himself bragging about Rogers and

Moulder, rising stars despite being white, honing his game and his will against tough, talented opposition.

Mid-August arrived and with it, two-a-day football practices, Kirkwood's team looking to shake off consecutive losing seasons. During that time, I played wide receiver and enjoyed lots of activity after we'd fall behind and then try to fling our way back into games. I'd even earned all-conference honors my junior year, thanks to late game touchdown catches heaved by quarterback Dave Gamble. Our improved outlook drew Tommy back onto the football field where he would achieve all-conference status as our starting safety. Jesse came out, too, playing high school football for the first time, but adapting so quickly he tore through opposing teams as a defender, the perfect size and speed to run through blockers and chase down backs. He tackled and disrupted, returning both a fumble and an intercepted pass for touchdowns en route to all-district honors, thereafter receiving attention from college football recruiters. We rose to a number five ranking in the St. Louis area before dropping a pair of late season games to finish 7–3, a memorable season and turnaround that just happened to delay our participation in basketball practice to a week before the season began.

Not that Mr. Miller minded. Unlike previous seasons during which he was forced to rummage through his roster searching for nuggets like a shopper at the Salvation Army, that year brought seasoned talent already meshed together by the previous year's improbable run to the Sweet Sixteen. All five starters returned, supported by a deep and athletic bench. His three senior starters arrived from the football field unscathed, familiar with his system, and in reasonably good condition (although football sprints were in no way comparable to basketball line drills and it always took me weeks to really catch my breath in hoop games). As we set up to practice as a unit for the first time, Mr. Miller enjoyed the luxury of stationing five skilled athletes in his full-court press: Bill, Rock, and I all former wide receivers, plus Tommy and Jesse, both former football defensive backs. In that respect, our varied summer activities, while lacking in fundamental basketball drills, had nevertheless bolstered our raw athleticism, empowering Mr. Miller as a recruiter given the pick of the recess mob, to select only the best and fastest, and to assign them the simple charter to run and run and play. He renounced decorum for chaos under the credo that his guys were more athletic than the other guy's, so we'd turn every game into a track meet, and always win.

Our success also came of what the five of us had in common: speed, athleticism, and playground outlooks that drew us together in a game where victory chose the most intrepid with nary a nod to grand plans or agendas. This granted us free reign over the contest and freedom from the outside world. Given the anonymity and innocence of youth, we played, frolicking through frantic practices with only Mr. Miller and Coach Mansinger as our witnesses; our station defined by the color of our reversible jerseys and not our skin; the steady cadence of whistle and hand claps driving us forward, faster, faster, faster. We were ahead of the competition and away from the crowd, any of whom might seek to deter us or plunge our faces into current events and reality. But we were so young and full of hope, devoid of our own prejudice and desperately avoiding everyone else's, such that we cleared the wash, gulping at fresh air, purified by the sun and wind, elements of innocence.

Three blacks and two whites, we were an alloy, a union of disparate elements stronger and more durable than its parts, our impurity the substance of our superiority, an unlikely, stubborn steel prevailing over pure iron or gold, a white/black blend optimized against all-black or all-white opponents. We were heated, mixed, and cured, emerging from the caldron galvanized, allied, and alloyed. It was like blending the pick of all players at the Center, and then taking on all comers, able to hold the court all day.

Mr. Miller sifted through his boundless bag of tricks and produced one wand, one spell with which to define our team: pace. He set that pace in practice, running us through successions of speed, layup drills where the ball never hit the floor; instead, it was snatched from the net and thrown ahead to a runner in stride, then two-on-one and three-on-two drills, constantly repeating ball movement in the open court to create easy shots. On defense, he controlled the pace with pressure, teaching us to relentlessly hound opposing ball handlers. He demonstrated to us that a defender placed at midcourt could reach any pass thrown from the backcourt to the frontcourt, especially if that defender was as lithe and athletic as Rock.

The root goal of a fast pace was to maximize the number of possessions in order to lengthen the game. Jack Nicklaus used to say that if he had to compete on a single hole, he'd want it to be a par five, the longest par five possible in order to maximize the number and quality of shots required to win. This would expose an opponent's weaknesses while optimizing Nicklaus' strengths. On a par three hole, one lucky shot could beat him. Following this same approach, Mr. Miller sought to expose our opponents' flaws, widening the battlefield and prompting conflict, ensuring victory for the better team. If opponents broke the press and then slowed down and pulled the ball out, great; we'd be spared any punishment. And if they did break through and then rush a shot, that was fine too because that would be just another possession for us. We were never chastised for a turnover on a pass to create a layup or easy bucket; pace was the rule. Make the game as long as you can and the better team will win. One losing coach lamented that his team might have caught Kirkwood, but the game ended too soon to which Mr. Miller responded, "Hell, you could play us all night and we'd still win."

We tore through the first week of practice, unified and omnipotent, a year stronger and smarter, our full-court press now equal parts precision and pandemonium. Tommy, Bill, and Jesse trapped upcourt, forcing desperate passes that were easy pickings for an athlete as long and smooth as Rock, while I defended the basket against any run outs, all of us reveling in the simplicity of it all. Then on a bitter cold morning, days before our first game, I staggered out of my bedroom to the breakfast table to find a copy of the *West County Journal* spread out to an article detailing Kirkwood's selection as the preseason number one team in the area and my selection as the number one player.

161

My parents smiled and watched me read, ten minutes of recognition followed by life as usual in a household where academics and citizenship drove and athletics rode in the back seat. We stuffed the paper away for good and I headed off to another day of school and practice. But our membrane had been penetrated, our snow globe shaken and cracked. It was just a small intrusion, a simple documentation of our potential, and validation of our hard work. But notoriety had come knocking, the first tiny pressure point in a season that would fill with them.

KHS starting five in white. Rogers shooting, #22 Moulder, #10 Grice, #30 Jackson, Rock on Charlie Shell's hip and in his ear.

Chapter 9

Third quarter ends and it's tied, 38–38. In our huddle, Mr. Miller repeats what we're to do: zone pressure up court and fall back into a zone. He's as animated as I've ever seen him, eyes wild and imploring. My mind wanders a bit to earlier games in the tournament, games we dominated, opponents we demoralized and sent packing. I look across at the Kirkwood crowd, clapping in sync with our cheerleaders who dance and leap in their wool uniforms, all of them active but apprehensive. Raytown's crowd hollers and revels like drunken sailors, aware of the drama, but devoid of concern.

UCLA wins the NCAA tournament just about every year. Coach Wooden gets the credit and no doubt he's the best coach out there, but he's also got the best talent. All twelve Bruins are superstars; Wooden just knows how to get them to play their roles. There's something else, though. Wooden says that in any prolonged, single-elimination tournament, a team is destined to play one bad game. There's no getting around it. It may be early or it may be the final, but you're going to play one bad game. So in order to win the tournament, you have to win that game. We wander out to start the fourth quarter and I know this is that game. Sure, Raytown's plan is working, but the fact is we're missing shots, missing free throws, and missing steals. If we were playing as well as last night, we'd be up ten. If we were playing as well as the Northwest game, we'd be up twenty. But we're not.

If this were the Center, I'd be scanning the sidelines looking to see who's got next, maybe even work my way over to tell him to pick me if we get beat. But it's not the Center and there's no next. We've gotta find a way to win this one.

For starters, there's the center jump. The ref tosses it over my head again, so I tip to Billy. There's no chance to break, so we walk it up. They sag inside and give Markle a seventeen-footer that's short. Plus that's not our shot. He's open, he has to take it, but it's their pace. Back they come and they're forcing it into Stolle. Number 40 passes up the jumper he's been taking all night and enters to Stolle and Rock bats it out of bounds. Second entry and Rock pressures a turnover. Billy dribbles it up, they overplay Rhein and Rock flashes into the key; pass, catch and make a ten-footer. Rock's alive and if he can find a rhythm, well, he's the wildcard. Raytown has no answer for him.

Rock just misses a steal off of our press and Stolle hurries a baseline jumper that's off. Rhein to the line, deep breath and he buries it. First three points of the quarter are ours but I know better than to think we're in control, not against this bunch. Number 40 pump-fakes Rhein into the air. Hmmm, strange, Rhein never leaves his feet. Number 40 dribbles inside and fires from the baseline but Rhein has landed and lunged and he flicks it off 40 and out of bounds. Our big man is playing huge. Billy comes back and draws a shooting foul, a miss and a make and now we're up four.

Does that constitute momentum, those four points? Hardly. A jumper and two free throws, not exactly the run and gun stakes we like to drive into opponents. Our crowd sits on the edges of their seats,

165

waiting, wishing for a true rally, ready to erupt. We're all antsy, trying to make something happen. I let 24 go baseline and swing my arm behind his dribble, looking for a clean steal but I foul him. Single free throw is good and in my haste I've given them a cheapie. Rock flashes to the same spot as his previous make, catch and shoot, but they've pushed out on him, just a small adjustment but enough that he misses. Then back on defense, Markle misses a steal, fouls 30 and he makes his free throw. Two points shaved off our lead and they never took a shot.

I can feel this thing slipping away from us. Six minutes left. They run a set play for 22 who catches it in the deep corner. Tough angle eighteen-foot baseline jumper is good. Tie game now. We can't make a shot. We're pressing up man to man all over the court. Tommy cuts 40 off just across midcourt, he picks up his dribble, nearly traveling and Billy just misses the steal as he hurtles past. They finally get it in to Stolle who pivots with a nifty head fake, Rock bites and Stolle goes under him for an easy layup. I had vowed to help out on Stolle but Rock's been stopping him. I could have contested that shot, I should have, but I didn't. It's like that dream where you are trying to run, trying to move, but you're swimming in air and can't. We're all a step slow now. Maybe the pressure of trying so hard to turn up the pace has worn us down.

Next time down Rhein is batting it back and forth off the backboard while Raytown players swat at it looking like kids jumping for a beach ball against their dad. The ref finally sends Rhein to the line for one, which he misses. Back on offense Raytown moves it smartly against our man pressure, no dribbling just a lot of passing and 40 pulls up along the baseline for a tough jumper that rattles around,

166

about to come off into my hands and I'm lining up an outlet and a fast break. But it bounces again and goes in.

We miss and so do they but when Rhein pulls down the rebound, his outlet to Tommy bounces off his hands and 24 is there to steal it. We're confused. Tommy drops his arms and glares at Rhein while Billy rubs his hands together and pressures the ball. Raytown calls timeout, three and a half minutes to go and now they're up four. Mr. Miller inserts Jesse for Rhein; our starting five back out there, our very best pressure group. Raytown lines up four in a row facing the inbounder and I glance around, Tommy on the inbounder with Billy, Rock and Jesse shoulder to shoulder with me. It's getting late.

The Storm

I see the bad moon arising
I see trouble on the way
I see earthquakes and lightnin'
I see bad times today
            –"Bad Moon Rising," Creedence Clearwater
Revival

On game days, we were required to wear a coat and tie to school, an inconvenience established to limit hallway hijinks and to shine the light of responsibility on us. But by the time Friday arrived, as we walked the halls like little gentlemen before our first game, the lofty expectations had spread and the school was alive with anticipation. We cast curious glances at each other all day; even the substitute players were treated like icons. One of my teachers began class with the question, "So, Drew, is the basketball team as good as they say?" I stared at my desk, shrugged my shoulders, and tugged at my shirt collar and tie. I'd thought we'd be pretty good, but not all that.

The bus ride over to opening night was loose, clusters of players talking and laughing, good-natured taunts all around. I sat in the locker room relishing the weekend, that night's game, the next morning at the Center, and the following night right back here. It didn't get much better than that. At guard, Bill The Thrill and Tommy Showtime. Sugar Bear at one forward and Rock at the other with me at center. My nickname was The Franchise, a moniker borrowed from Kareem Abdul Jabbar when he was still Lew Alcindor, playing for the Milwaukee Bucks. I wasn't the one-man team that Alcindor was but I was grabbing a lot of headlines so the nickname stuck. A locker room brimming with tons of athleticism, experience and confidence, no thought about a season or a title, just tonight's game. Go out there and run them off the floor.

We destroyed our two opponents to win the Maplewood Tournament. Bill and I earned all-tournament honors; Rock earned tournament MVP. He accepted his trophy sheepishly, dropping his head, and thrusting the trophy into the air as the Kirkwood contingent cheered, clapped, and stared. I was happy for him and relieved that a teammate was chosen as top dog, already conscious of the potential divisiveness that lay with personal success and notoriety. I was a middle child, a natural arbitrator with the team, and that season had brought my greatest challenges to date. The all-tournament team numbered

168

only five, leaving just two spots for members of the other three teams and none for Tommy or Jesse, both of whom were good enough but were limited by the short practice time following football and by simple arithmetic—one ball, five players, two quarters of play before garbage time. There just weren't enough opportunities for all of us to star in every game. I glanced at the others as we headed for the locker room, Jesse marveling at Rock and his trophy, and Tommy shuffling in silence staring straight ahead.

Tommy wasn't selfish, but he carried all those expectations. School mornings, I'd walk the icy path between buildings and pass by the brothers, ten or fifteen of them huddled together in their leather coats, leaning against the wind like trees, talking and laughing. Sometimes Tommy would look over and nod, but mostly he stayed hunkered down, and maybe one or two of the others would glance my way. I imagined them pressing Tommy, "Boy, you should be scoring all the points instead of him," "How come all you do is throw it to white folks instead of shooting it?" I knew Tommy well enough not to worry about him succumbing, but winning games had become so easy now. His competitiveness must have ebbed a little, creating a vacuum for personal goals to occupy whether they belonged to him or his friends. Tommy had worked hard and contributed greatly, but most of the headlines belonged to me or to Bill. This was Tommy's senior year, and he knew that when the season ended, so would his hoop career. Get 'em while you can...

Jesse was still the keen, innocent little kid he'd always been, no agenda and no envy. But he followed Tommy's lead, abdicating his own moods for Tommy's. If Tommy had a good game, they both smiled and sang on the bus; but if Tommy felt slighted and sulked, so did Jesse, starting to join the song and catching Tommy's eye, and then falling silent, biting his lip and puckering up to contain himself. It was like water creeping into the cracks, clear and docile, but still a solvent, slowly and invisibly eating away at the foundation. The competition of the previous year's games and the last-second desperation rallies were long gone, and with them the unity and commitment fostered by the game. The guys in the other uniforms offered precious little challenge now, so hearts and minds began to wander, cracks widening.

But there would be no fissures if Mr. Miller had anything to do with it, no idle time, no fertile ground in which to sow the seeds of dissent. Practices were nonstop track meets, the ball whipping around, made shots yanked from the net and fired down court, run out on offense, and hustle back on D, pressing every chance we got.

We spent hours a day pressing and breaking pressure ensuring proficiency with both. As our pressure improved Mr. Miller would test our court coverage against six players, then seven, and ultimately eight, forcing us to play the ball and any conceivable passing angle, honing both our athleticism and teamwork. By the time we took the court against opposing teams guarding five of them felt easy to the point of unfair. Jesse would slide in front, feet spread, palms facing upward, a smack-talking square of flypaper, constricting and inescapable, too quick to avoid and too strong to beat. Even if teams passed over or around us for a while they could never sustain it. Their patience and resolve were invariably broken for just a minute or two during which we'd steal it, pass ahead, score and get right back in their grill as they'd glance to the scoreboard at an ever-increasing deficit and draw halting breaths like bathers on an icy shore.

High school teams typically practiced three days a week for two or three hours a day during which they worked on the myriad elements necessary to simply field a team and play together on the floor, leaving little or no time to practice against pressure. That's why SLUH had tormented us so in that game my sophomore year. We had never practiced against a press so we were incompetent. Furthermore, unless a team is an accomplished pressing team there is no way to simulate real pressure. It's like the fire drills in elementary school, a simple, boring exercise of lining up and marching outside, paying little attention to much besides seeing how long we could stay out there in lieu of class time. Kids were oblivious to the true intent of the drill and gaining no real value because it wasn't real. The same went for any team trying to emulate our pressure in their practice, they couldn't. So when we would first set up and jump a pass we'd see that same look in each opponent's eye, a look of fear, uncertainty and doubt. We were a pain in the butt to play against.

As enjoyable as it was to trap, steal and fast break, Mr. Miller had a lot more in mind than just rolling the ball out there

171

and unleashing his dogs. He knew he had superior athletes so a fast pace left opposing coaches with just two choices. The first was to engage the speed and try to run with us, in effect, trading baskets. But this was disastrous, as we would always win a race. The second was to slow things down, limit possessions and hope to keep things close. But in a game like that, the three or four steals and run outs we would invariably create were always the difference, ultimately forcing teams to play catch up and right into our hands.

I had learned some things my junior year and one was the risk-reward equation that came with blocking shots. I was now 6-foot-6 with decent hops and a good chance to block most players' shots. However certain refs were prone to call fouls on such plays, especially short refs who to me must have been guards, if they had even played at all. As such they seemed sympathetic to a smaller player's plight against a shot blocker. I imagined them inventing contact in their minds and purposely tagging me with unjust foul calls.

Right or wrong, I changed my approach for my senior year, deciding to draw charging fouls by stepping out in front of approaching dribblers rather than leaping to contest their shot. This decision began to pay immediate dividends as these guards-turned-refs seemed to relate to a tactic available to players big or small and designed to mute athleticism. I began amassing dozens of charging calls that not only penalized the guilty player, it discouraged further sorties into the lane for fear of more such calls. I had mixed feelings about this approach, a practice that would be challenged and taunted at the Center. But if it kept me out of foul trouble and gave our team an edge then I was certainly prepared to swallow a little pride and play the game the way officials called it. I could only hope Loose Booty wouldn't wander into one of our games and witness my sellout to The Game.

Drawing charges bred familiarity with most officials, middle aged sports guys, many of whom coached football or other high school sports, local guys who had officiated KHS games for many years and mine in particular for three or four years and so knew me pretty well. I had always been polite, raising my hand dutifully when whistled for a foul, keeping my mouth shut and not complaining about calls. By my senior year I would chat with them, "Mr. Sanders, we're going to call timeout after this free throw," or "Mr. Davidson, Number 33 is holding me, can you please keep an eye on that next time down?"

It worked with every ref except one, John Schnell. He coached football at one of our rivals, Parkway Central, so maybe he had it in for me as an opposing football player, but he never gave me the charge call. Never. I'd slide in front of a dribbler, absorb the contact, take the obligatory fall to the floor and look up hopefully only to see him whistling and hopping past, hands on hips and shaking his head to signal a blocking foul against me. I'd struggle to my feet and dust myself off, knowing better than to challenge him openly and instead looking down at the floor or off into the distance to avoid attracting any undue attention. I'd say quietly, "Gee Mr. Schnell, I really thought I got there in time," or "Mr. Schnell, I guess I was still moving." Sometimes I'd even ask, "Mr. Schnell, I'm not arguing that one, but can you tell me what I did wrong so I don't do it on the next one?" It was all to no avail. I began to think he'd call a block just to see what I'd do or say, collecting my little pleas like butterflies in a net. It was my first experience with salesmanship and a customer who was never going to buy.

My little recruitment of officials was merely a distraction to an otherwise unrelenting assault on opposing teams. Our second team could beat most first teams - not a boast, just fact. We brought six-foot-eight Rhein Dabler, six-foot-five Steve Schaper and six-foot-three Sam Weaver off the bench. Any of them would have started for any team we played. Junior guard Scott Markle rotated with our two starting guards and would start himself a year later. Most practices were faster, tougher and more challenging than games, our success a direct result of the quality of our reserves.

Early in the season we remained cautious and determined, approaching the Vianney game and Charlie Shell with trepidation and then entering our conference season expecting tough games from several teams including Lindberg and Parkway Central. All three teams came in undefeated and we annihilated them all. By the time we entered the Normandy Christmas Tournament, we were 10–0 and only one team had come within twenty points of us. We were the top seed in the tournament, riding a wave of confidence with no concern for an early exit and subsequent Christmas practices. As the top seed, we drew marquee game times, evening affairs that were well attended, the arena seating filled with KHS fans as well as area hoop fans there to see what all the buzz was about.

Night games were new to us. Most games my sophomore and junior years were matinee events staged among low seeds before polite gatherings of fans and families. But now we took the floor to roaring ovations, reveling in the spotlight introductions on darkened floors, hand bumps and back slaps all around before shedding our warm-ups and going to work, victimizing our frightened prey like lions in a gladiator arena. Bus rides home were raucous and loose, huddled together in small clusters or hollering up and down the aisle until somebody noticed that we were passing by the Olympic Theatre, an anachronistic drive-in that showed X-rated movies at a time before the Internet or DVDs, rendering its fare rare to the point of legendary. Our sudden discovery felt all the more unique given that our previous trips had been in daylight, during which the "Big O" had lain dormant, but now, finally, there it was, lit up and brightly flashing its titillating images, fifty feet across, a glimmer between the trees and visible for just a short stretch of road. The shout of "Hey, look at that!" was followed by the thundering feet of a dozen hormone-raging teenaged boys, hurling themselves against the left side of the bus with such force and timing that the bus rocked up on two wheels. The driver let out an expletive-laced tirade producing no bearing on our lascivious leers, as the bus finally settled, the giant screen slipped out of sight, and a hushed voice croaked wistfully, "Is tomorrow's game a night game, too?"

We blew out all four opponents in winning the Normandy Tournament and continued into the New Year thrashing opponents by ever widening scores. Newspaper

175

stories continued to chronicle our success and a local TV station appeared after one practice to interview several of us, which had everyone scurrying home to catch that night's newscast. Around town, folks would stop us to congratulate us and wish us well and when we'd attend another team's game the crowd would hush when we passed through. We were conquering heroes just about everywhere but at the Center where each of us played individually, joining up with whoever had winners, opposing each other as often as teaming together. The Center gang ignored our high school team's success, treating us as a parent would a child, proud but unimpressed.

There were times when racial lines were obscured, when the game wove its thread among us, precision pressing and passing, joining us in the vanquishing of another opponent. We'd sit on the bench, watching our subs widen the lead to thirty or forty, and bathe in the collective admiration and adulation showered upon us. There had been times when our stations proved more identical than diverse, like once when I fainted outside the junior high gym after a three-hour session of games. I was thirteen, dressed in school clothes, and wearing desert boots because I didn't have basketball clothes or sneakers. I was half-starved since I'd passed on the previous night's casserole and risen Saturday to a phone call beckoning me to some hoops. I bolted out the door on an empty stomach and played nonstop until retiring to the hall to phone for a ride. I woke on the floor, everyone staring down at me, and one father said simply, "We'll stop at Burger King on the way home." I was just another kid—black or white—of limited means, completely giving in to the game.

I played my freshman season in cheap tennis shoes, soles so worn that I slid to stops, the bottoms so thin I blistered the balls of both feet to the point of blood and infection. That was all I had until my call up to varsity, prompting my ninth grade coach and team to pony up to buy me my first pair of Converse All Star sneakers, preserving my skin while forcing me to adjust to sudden stops and change of direction like an old man mastering a new sports car.

These were facets of the game and youth and circumstance that could just as likely have affected a black kid as they had me. My parents never knew I'd passed out because by the time I was dropped off at my house, I'd consumed several cheeseburgers and a large soda. But where my experiences were largely ignored—they were stereotypically assumed with blacks. I got a big dose of such typecasting during my senior hoop season.

Bucky Givens was a talented, multi-sport athlete at Webster Groves High School. He began playing varsity sports as a freshman, so by the time he was a senior, other teams had seen so much of him they presumed he'd been held back in school several times. His tenure, reinforced by his full beard and Afro, plus the fact that he was black, stimulated lots of sarcastic insults like he had kids old enough to attend his games. I was a sophomore during Givens senior season. I never joined in the taunts, but I did figure Bucky was older and must have been held back in school. Then one evening, during my senior year, our varsity players loitered in the hallway at Parkway Central looking at the trophy cases and listening to the B team sneakers squeak up and down the floor inside the abandoned gym. A Parkway cheerleader shyly approached Rock and me and asked, "Are you the Kirkwood team?" We nodded confidently, our fame gaining us yet another audience. She stepped past me and asked Rock, "Are you Drew Rogers?" He shot me a look of bewilderment as I seized the moment.

"Yes, he is," I chirped, stepping beside them. "And I'm Robert Williams." Ignoring me, she turned back to Rock.

"I've heard of you. They say you've never graduated and you just keep playing."

And there it was. I had become Bucky Givens with a twist. This white Parkway Central cheerleader assumed not only that I was old and stupid, but that I was black. Rock and I laughed all the way to the locker room, but when the game started, the fans knew who I was. They let me have it with the same taunts, and although we blew them out and silenced their crowd, another crack in our foundation had emerged. Rock was perceptive and he felt the stereotype.

Not that Rock was beyond reproach. A loner, he remained in character at school, roaming the hallways instead of sitting in class, falling behind in his studies to the point that all of us worried about his eligibility. Mr. Miller found him wandering one day and took swift action. He met with each of Rock's teachers to begin monitoring his progress, enrolling him in his math class where he slowly and subtly recruited him to the material, kind but fair. Rock ultimately earned a passing grade and newfound respect for his mentor. He started spouting the mantra, "That man taught me how to count my money!"

I don't suppose I was being taught much by then, safely tucked away in a senior curriculum of electives. I'd previously passed the classes required for graduation and therefore cavorted in subjects like the History of Sports, my day nicely broken up by study hall sessions held in the school cafeteria, the hour before lunch time, Hostess cupcakes covered in linen, out of sight but so inviting, a tantalizing ten feet from where I sat. I was both starving and mischievous. So it wasn't long before Albert Roos and I began timing the class monitor's walks through the tables, pouncing on one pack each when she would round the far corner, devouring the cakes in two gulps to the amusement of our fellow students, and tossing the packages into the trash before she returned. We were clever, but inexperienced, violating multiple credos of the practiced thief, like never return to the scene of a crime, and avoid witnesses. Unbeknownst to us, the monitor emptied the trash can, made her rounds, and then returned, calmly removing the plastic cover to fish out our Hostess wrappers. She dropped them on our table then led us to the principal's office for my first yellow slip not signed by Mrs. Parham, who, had she learned of this episode, would surely have nodded, thrust her finger in my face, and said, "I knew you'd never turn out to be anything."

Success and complacency seemed to impact Rock in their own way, magnifying the depth and frequency of his moods, moping and sulking through some games, and then flourishing in and dominating others. He was a lightning rod for

179

criticism, taunting opposing players, snapping at referees, and ignoring our pleas to play hard. We wondered if his inconsistencies were caused by alcohol or drugs, never knowing that he was simply acting out resentment at his siblings for disrespecting his mother, a child in a man's body, frustrated and angry.

A month into the season it was clear we had something special as throngs of fans confidently awaited each blowout. Newspapers hungered for inside stories to spruce up the mundane reports of wide margin victories, soon settling on two topics: my hair and Mr. Miller's unrequited quest for a state title, each mildly entertaining and distracting at the same time.

I had grown my hair over my ears and curling down the back of my neck at a time when short hair was still the rule among most athletes and long hair was the province of hippies and rebels. A few sportswriters featured it as some radical expression, a perspective they leveraged against growing boredom with our success while I simply sought a different look. I continued to grow it out and the topic's interest abated considerably.

Mr. Miller's 38-year quest for the golden plaque proved a much more compelling and enduring story, surfacing early in the season and reaching a crescendo in January when he coached his one thousandth game, all at KHS, establishing marks for both loyalty and longevity. Reporters would press microphones into his face and stand scribbling away in notebooks, pestering him with questions about his career until the topic gravitated to his failure at ever winning a state title. This would draw an inevitable shrug and dismissal from Mr. Miller which only served to increase the persistence from the avid scribes until they could extract a grudging admission of unfulfilled dreams, whether a stated admission or hopeless shake of the head.

In an effort at self-deprecating modesty he would sometimes wax philosophical about what it takes to win a title and what his chances were with his current team. Most times he would dismiss our team as too dependent on pressure when the key to winning was straight-up man-to-man defense and a set offense, effectively overpowering other teams. I read about these admissions, because he never said such to our faces, and wonder why in the world he would coach us to play one way while dismissing it as a weakness. But then I'd remember how many times he had won cat-and-mouse games and figure he was just instructing all the other coaches how they should play, knowing that his way and his team were the best.

One doubt that did arise was why Mr. Miller failed to intervene with our black players. In my mind the only thing that could possibly stop us were personal agendas, Tommy's potential for selfishness and Rock's continuous mood swings in particular. If he was such a great coach, the very best to my way of thinking, then why couldn't he or wouldn't he fix things? Was he oblivious? Did he choose to ignore it and hope it would go away?

What I failed to consider at the time was the situation. Blacks had just recently begun to participate in KHS athletics. There were still a lot of pent up prejudices among school employees, parents and fans. Was it right to intervene with a black athlete's behavior if it wasn't demonstrably detrimental to the team? And were the white players above reprimand? What about my hair? But at that time I figured we were still kids and he was the adult, the veteran coach, the pro. Here we stood, facing a chance to win most if not all of our games, to win that elusive championship, the topic of so much hand wringing and angst. Mr. Miller possessed all of that experience and perspective and just needed to fix the one chink in our armor.

I was never particularly close with Mr. Miller, probably because I had never lacked for a lot of what he offered. I was raised in a two-parent family with a loving and exacting father, a constant and prevalent force in my life. I had church ministers, scout leaders and various other coaches providing mentoring and grounding. I was set. I had honed my skills on neighbors' baskets and various informal hoop venues, a product of repetition and exploration more than any coaching. Mr. Miller motivated and taught me but never really touched me. And he probably recognized that his time and efforts were better spent with players in greater need.

Bill shared with Mr. Miller a keen insight and an unquenchable thirst for the game. Bill was a coach on the floor and a vehicle through which Mr. Miller could deploy all of his knowledge and innovations. Bill would listen and understand, implement and even improve. He must have been an incredible gift to a coach like Mr. Miller, like that one person in the room who gets your jokes and is laughing out loud even before you hit the punch line.

Bill and I had live-at-home fathers actively raising us, in stark contrast to Jesse and Robert. Neither of them had fathers in their lives. Tommy's father was a mystery. It's not like Showtime sat around the locker room and told us his life story, but we had come to know that his father, though living, was not around much and certainly not done up in red and white and singing the KHS fight song. Jesse's mother was incredibly energetic and devoted, a constant presence at games and a strict guide for all of her sons. So Jesse remained grounded and whole. Tommy had developed a will and discipline of his own, traits at which he worked each day leaving little time or room for an alternate father figure.

Rock was the one for whom Mr. Miller filled a void. Rock reeked of apathy, inviting immense concern among his teammates while secretly craving attention and love from Mr. Miller. Rock never knew his father and then grew up too quickly while chasing his older brothers. Finally presented with a man who listened, cared and stuck around, he was hooked. Some of Rock's antics were self-destructive but the governor of all that, the single force that forever kept Rock's knife drawn but never to his own throat was Mr. Miller. In hindsight I now realize that Mr. Miller had a lot on his plate, from the exorcism of his own state championship demons to the still inchoate prospect of playing blacks and whites on the floor while fending off racism in the stands. Still, at that time I was anxious, my constant focus on the game threatened by distractions I felt were solvable by my coach.

Selfishness and greed were annoyances to me, folds of The Game, intruding but benign. None of us ever held a pass or forced a shot to our own benefit, as stats and glory were the stuff of hallway conversations and post-game pouts, but not actions. Jesse and Tommy played their roles consistently and well, combining with Bill and me to form a solid base with which we could beat most teams most of the time. We emerged as the best team that the Kirkwood school system could produce. Left to ourselves, we probably would have won twenty or so games and gone deep into the state tournament. But we were destined to achieve more than that because, like most preeminent teams, we had an X-factor, a wildcard, a transfer. Rock fell out of the sky onto our team, at once enigmatic and magical. He was that rare player with ability as limitless as it was unpredictable, a volatile combination that troubled us all.

I don't know if we needed a wake-up call, but when our record reached 14-0, we got one. It was late January and I had no idea if Northwest was watching us, but we sure watched them. They were still undefeated and ranked number one. We'd taken domination to another level, now winning all games by thirty or more points, culminating in a win at Ladue that ended in a double blowout—both the winning score and my right ankle. It was my first and only thirty-point game, which is probably why Mr. Miller left me in for the fourth quarter, and as I scored an uncontested layup for points thirty-two and thirty-three, I rolled my right ankle. That ankle was weak—I had sprained it twice during football—and I came down on it with all my weight. That impact combined with the low-top red Converse sneakers we all wore, which provided no more ankle support than house slippers, resulted in severely torn ligaments, a cast for three weeks, and uncertainty about when I might return.

The team, however, never missed a beat, winning all six games I missed as Tommy, Rock, and Bill took turns running up big scoring nights. My emotions ran bittersweet as I felt happy for my team and teammates, but anxious to play, all the while chided by newspaper headlines like, "Kirkwood Wins. Drew Who?" I was relegated to watching games from the team bench, wearing my worn corduroy sport coat, dated shirt with the tight collar, and faded tie, my voice so hoarse from hollering I borrowed a duck call from Don Bertram. He dubbed it the lame duck call in deference to my wounded condition. I honked that thing nonstop until an official complained and our school principal rendered it a dead duck call. I got my cast off the next day.

Mr. Miller gushed that the team had grown in my absence so we'd be stronger when I returned, but I wasn't so sure. My ankle was purple and so swollen on the outside that my foot pronated inward making me pigeon-toed. And it hurt like hell. Following a week of alternating ice and scalding heat, plus a few tentative practices, into a game I went. I came off the bench before an excited KHS crowd, my ankle heavily taped, but still wearing those red slippers, sore but mindful of my father's words not to limp or make excuses. I heeded him even when I badly airballed my first shot. The team had grown, Bill ripping off 24 points while I scored only six in another blowout win. I had nearly a month of games to regain my touch and to

185

assimilate back with the team. We closed the regular season with a rare Friday night and Saturday night pair of games, which didn't deter us from playing at the Center that Saturday morning, play that was dramatically more challenging than the two high school games combined. Eight hours of hoop over a twenty-four-hour period were a piece of cake for our young bodies. We had disproved Mr. Miller's prediction that we would lose a game, and his caution that it might even be better to lose one than to carry a season-long win streak into the state tournament. We were oblivious to history or other factors, simply beating anyone put before us (except Loose Booty that Saturday morning who lit me up like a roman candle while Rock kept carping, "Who's *got* him?").

We were 25–0. Northwest had finally lost a game, but they still held the number one ranking in the St. Louis area and the state as we entered the state regionals. It would take seven wins to claim the championship, but one win to make our season: a win against the Northwest Blue Devils.

Chapter 10

They damn near don't get it inbounded but at the last second Stolle darts forward to receive it. Rock harasses him and he picks his dribble up just in time to avoid Billy's swipe. Then they stall. It's legal because they're ahead now. Thirty seconds pass before I get a piece of an entry pass intended for Stolle, tipping it up toward our guards. Tommy's crouched to grab it but Stolle never gives up on the play, leaping out to swat it out to midcourt and his own guards.

Another twenty seconds expire but then Jesse overwhelms 40, knocks it loose and picks it up. Two minutes to go, we've got to get a good look. But we don't and Billy fouls on the rebound and 30 makes the free throw. It's a cheap foul call and the thought crosses my mind to grab the ball and stare at the floor, tapping my foot in protest of the call but we're a long way from the Center and we can't shame them into anything. Raytown knows how to draw fouls and they make their foul shots. They'd be one and done at the Center but in a state championship game they're right at home. We miss, Rock fouls and 22 hits the free throw to put them up, 48-42, completing a 10-0 run. Well not exactly a run: four minutes, six free throws, two baskets and a bunch of Kirkwood turnovers and missed shots. Dull but effective.

I grab a rebound, outlet to Billy, a single dribble and he finds Jesse down court, Jesse executes a nifty spin dribble and a fade away twelve-footer that's good. Finally! We're back within four. They reach

187

the frontcourt just ahead of a ten count and begin to stall. Tommy tries the same swat from behind that I did with the same result, free throws to Raytown. Tommy punches the air and then flings both arms in disgust. It's the bonus situation now and 30 makes both ends of the one-and-one. A minute and a half to go and it's 50-44, bad guys.

Rock misses a free throw but Jesse bats it into the air. Rock snatches it and nails a ten-footer in the lane. Back within four, still plenty of time. They're into the frontcourt and stalling again. Another precious thirty seconds evaporates and then Jesse traps his man on the sideline and steals it clean. He's off to the races but his layup hits the bottom of the rim. Raytown is whistled for a foul in the ensuing melee and on our next possession Tommy is fouled in the act of shooting. I remember that arm fling and know he's not nervous, just pissed. I stand along the lane in rebound position facing Rock across from me. "Come on!" Rock shouts, glancing across at me. Tommy buries the first one and Rock leans into the lane furiously clapping his hands. They hand it to Tommy for his second free throw and Rock shakes his fists at Tommy. "Come on!"

I've wondered all season long just how much Rock cares. Half the time he was a no show and most other times he was detached, seemingly indifferent. I'd lie in bed at night and say to myself that these games and this season were such an opportunity for all of us but especially for them. All that awaits Tommy and Jesse after this season is the Center. Rock has his senior season left but after that I figure not much more. I assume that for Rock there will be no college, no more organized games, no more cheering crowds, no more attention and glory. Granted, these are facets of the Game but we have always distilled things down to the game and I have to admit the accouterments of the Game oftentimes augment the game. Now Tommy toes the line desperately trying to shoot us back in and Rock stands there willing with all his might for Tommy to make this shot and give us a chance. The second free throw's good, 1:03 to go and back within two.

We're pressing all over the floor with everything we've got and Raytown blinks, a backcourt violation and possession back to us. Nearly a minute left, plenty of time. The next forty seconds are a blur. Time has suddenly sped up, the game getting away from us. We fight it, frantically throwing ourselves around, clawing for the ball and hoisting it back up. Jesse misses a jumper but Tommy draws a foul on the rebound. Tommy misses a jumper and Rock rebounds, quickly putting it back up. I can see it's going to rim out and I'm up in front of the rim, hands inches from the ball for an easy tip in, but incredibly it hangs for an extra split second, tantalizingly close but off limits until it clears the iron and as it does I'm fading back down and just can't snatch it. Out of bounds to Kirkwood, :35 left on the clock. We call timeout and set up a simple play with Jesse taking it out right under our basket with the option to lob to me or hit Rock cutting to the opposite side. Either one will be a great look.

We break the huddle and I fight the urge to sprint to my spot, lest I give away our intent. But hell, Geppetto's no dummy. This is Kirkwood's last chance. Don't let their leading scorer beat you. We set up and I draw a deep breath. Time should have slowed down by now but it hasn't, everything's still a rush. I step to my position but they've already handed Jesse the ball and the ref is into his five-count. I'm supposed to pick for Rock and then turn inside but Jesse makes eye contact with me and that's the signal. I have to jump because he's

189

tossing it up there. His pass is high where no one else can reach it and up I go.

Sparkle

Everybody's talkin' at me
I can't hear a word they're saying
Only the echoes in my mind
      –"Everybody's Talkin'", Fred Neil (Sung by
Harry Nilsson)

We beat St. Charles on Monday night in the round of sixteen, right back at Meramec Junior College where we had bowed out against Bayless the previous year. We played poorly, unable to shake them and it was still a one-point game late before we finally pulled away. I played particularly poorly, foul trouble early and then committing my fifth foul on a failed attempt to draw a charge. There was contact and as I sat on the floor clearing my head I failed to raise my hand when whistled and so was called for a technical foul to boot. I sat on the bench in a fog and caught the wrath of Mr. Miller afterwards, so disconsolate on the bus ride home it was Rock of all people trying to cheer me up in the parking lot.

Quite a few KHS fans loitered in the darkened lot and word quickly spread that Northwest had won its game in a blowout. Driving home it sank in. After an entire season of posturing and musing, of newspaper debates over which of us

190

might prevail, after countless hours scheming with Bill during free period on how we might match up, the streets had emptied for the duel. It would be Northwest and Kirkwood, Number One versus Number Two, city versus county.

Northwest dropped a late season game to Vashon yet still entered the state tournament rated number one. That loss was no embarrassment. Vashon was the defending state champion and featured Lamont Turner, a six-foot-seven monster headed for the University of Missouri on a basketball scholarship. But it did foretell two phenomena that would resurface in our game; the weak play of Northwest's guards and the potential for postgame violence.

During that earlier game, Northwest had led Vashon by six points with less than a minute to go. But the Blue Devils then committed five straight turnovers, the Northwest guards wilting under full court pressure from Vashon. Some coaches prefer to take a loss in the regular season to alleviate the pressure of an unbeaten streak but in so doing Northwest's Achilles heel was exposed. I'm sure Denver Miller took note.

Immediately following the Vashon game, Northwest players headed straight for their bus as fights began to break out among fans. Both teams were predominantly black so these skirmishes were territorial and not racial but were nevertheless a sign of the times. If you had issues with events you took to the streets and wrought havoc. Vashon fans were letting Northwest bunch know they weren't welcome in their neighborhood and despite the fact that Vashon had won the game, their fans still assaulted the Northwest team. The mob

191

inflicted so much damage to the Northwest bus it was incapacitated leaving frightened, bewildered Northwest players to find their individual rides home. All the while the Blue Devils imagined how much worse the assault might have been had they actually beaten Vashon.

Wednesday was game day. The newspaper heralded the game as a summit meeting, two titans entering an arena from which only one would emerge victorious. The KHS halls were abuzz as students rushed to purchase tickets for a game that was sure to sell out that night. The site would be Kiel Auditorium, smack in the middle of downtown St. Louis, just three miles away from Northwest High School and a dark and foreboding destination for a bunch of county white kids. My classmates took to forming groups for that night and most planned to discard their letter jackets lest they draw the attention of Northwest toughs.

I walked toward the cafeteria at lunchtime, skirting the area near the principal's office known as Hollywood and Vine, an area virtually off limits to whites. There had been fights there, blacks defending a small piece of turf against whites. One white football player was once beaten so badly he missed an ensuing game. This was the province of the black girls, the sisters, who were more feared than the black guys because they were much more confrontational. Most days they would have glared at me, perhaps even threatened me but today they shared the electric anticipation we all felt. Thus inspired, one of them approached and took my arm to walk with me. "Hey Drew," she purred. "You ever been with a black girl?" I kept walking. "I seen everything these black boys got and now I'm wondering about white boys, about you." In the next ten hours we were both going to stop wondering about me. Tomorrow I'd be cheered throughout Hollywood and Vine or banished forever.

I glanced at my new escort, eager and radiant, but deadly. I had no capacity for curiosity or attraction because I was afraid of her, at this moment a lone fox, beguiling and tempting but still a member of a potentially vicious pack. I twisted away and quickened my pace. There was enough to worry about tonight's game without adding any more intrigue.

Jesse burst from the pack and caught me, breathless and animated, begging me to stop and listen. "Drew, you think we can beat these guys tonight?" For all the speculation around this game, no one had yet asked me that question point blank. So I had never really considered it. I pondered it for all the time any teenager ponders anything, about three seconds.

"Yeah," I shrugged, continuing my walk.

"Those girls all say we'll lose. They say we can't beat those city niggers." Lunch period lasted forty minutes. Ten of my minutes were now gone. Five more and the cafeteria would be cleaned out of burgers and Hostess Cup Cakes. I was hungrier than I was concerned about Northwest. I was thinking about Maslow's hierarchy of needs at that point but was confused; maybe it was Pavlov's dog. I knew I was salivating but my poor grasp of the material in Psychology class left me addled. I kept walking but when Jesse presses there is no escape, just ask any of our opponents. "What do you think?" he persisted.

I stopped dead and faced my teammate, my cohort if not outright friend for the past five years. He looked at me, wide eyed and lathered. Hell, I wouldn't want him guarding me. "What do *you* think?" I responded.

He shook his head, confused as lunch time continued to slip away. I thought about the cafeteria orange juice, sitting in glasses for hours so that by the time my lunch period arrived, all the orange sat on the bottom and clear water on the top, divorced by time and gravity, never to be rejoined no matter how much you stirred. If you didn't get a burger you were left with mystery meat or overcooked spaghetti, stretchy and unbreakable with a half-life of one hundred years.

"Jesse, if I don't eat right now we have no chance." He looked like a kicked puppy. "Hey," I added. "We'll be fine, don't worry." He stared back, now eager and hopeful. "Those girls don't know anything," I added. "They've never seen Northwest. They're full of..." I caught myself and we both turned to see if any of them had heard and then bolted in opposite directions just in case they had.

We assembled that evening inside the KHS gym in preparation for the bus ride out to Kiel and I entered to find players standing in silence, alone or in pairs, heads down and hands thrust in their pockets. Mr. Miller stood by the door, pacing. Tommy's dad had been knifed. No one told me outright but somehow everyone knew. There were no details. When? How? Was his dad killed or wounded? I glanced at Tommy, standing stoically off to the side by himself, staring into the rafters and rocking slowly from foot to foot. I wondered about

194

his dad, who he was, what he was like. Was he some sort of criminal? How had he come to meet such a fate? But there were no answers. The news hung in the air like smoke after a fireworks display, colorless but acrid. If my dad had suffered an accident, Mr. Miller would have known, he'd have consoled me and then announced the details to the team so we could come together. This rumor had driven us to far corners of the gym, divided by our differing home lives. Black players shook their heads, knowing it just as likely could have been one of their families. White players struggled to comprehend it at all. We boarded the bus like mourners in a line.

The ride out to Kiel that night was as quiet as Mrs. Parham's classroom. Thoughts of Tommy's dad slowly gave way to anticipation of the game. I stared out the window as dusk fell and suburban lawns morphed into urban buildings and then into downtown tenements. I was subject to the same trepidation Jesse had felt heading into the Missouri countryside, in reverse. No one concerned himself with the state tournament or the potential trip to the Final Four. It was just a game, just this game, a chance to play a great team in a threatening venue and the incumbent risk of losing.

The walk from the bus inside to our locker room felt like an introduction to prison life, new meat walking among hardened prisoners. Clusters of blacks eyed us malevolently, some mouthing off. We dropped off our gear and sat in the stands to watch the start of the preceding quarterfinal game, leaving at half time to dress and prepare. We laced up, trying hard to ignore the distinct smell of marijuana smoke pervading

195

our locker room. We were nervous and distracted until Mr. Miller broke the ice. "Well it smells like someone was getting *up* for their game," he joked. This was the St. Louis University locker room. Sam Williams dressed here for college games and now his youngest brother, Rock sat staring into Sam's locker. Meanwhile Sam sat in the stands waiting to cheer his brother, that backyard abandonment of Rock a distant memory.

I was way beyond wondering how our blacks might compete with city blacks. The previous year's Sumner game and a whole lot of hard work and team growth left no doubt they would play well, we all would. I thought back to the summer before ninth grade when an impromptu game of tackle football arose among three friends and myself. Seth Whitman and I had kicked off to John Spence who was the broadest, strongest guy our age. Spence ran it back right at me and suddenly I was faced with putting a shoulder into this runaway bull or backing off and trying an arm tackle, effectively utter surrender. If Seth didn't dive in right behind me I was toast either way. There was just a split second to consider options and outcomes, a brief moment of doubt. Would Seth back me up? I drove into Spence with everything I had, praying for help and half a second later I felt Seth over the top of me, driving his shoulder in. The next thing I knew we were rolling over Spence and establishing ourselves against his strength and power. My trust had been rewarded then and would be now. Win or lose I trusted my teammates the same way.

The Vashon experience had steeled the Northwest Blue Devil team as they took the floor to face us and it had riled their crowd, this night the unofficial home team protecting their turf against the mostly white county crowd. I glanced at our opponents during warm-ups, going about their business, focused on the game, just like that Mathew Dickey football team back in eighth grade. They were trying as hard as we were to simply play the game and divorce themselves from fans and agendas.

Hercle "Poison" Ivy was the Northwest star, en route to St. Louis Player of the Year honors and a full ride to Iowa State where he would one day lead the Big Eight in scoring. A six-foot-three senior forward, he possessed a deadly jump shot and a scoring average around 25 points per game. His high arching shot was unblockable and intimidating for no doubt it had been honed against athletic leapers. If he could score on those inner city athletes, I wondered, who were we to stand against him.

It wouldn't be "we" at all. It would be Jesse. Mr. Miller put us in a box-and-one zone defense with four of us guarding spots and Jesse hounding Ivy all over the floor. I think Jesse was still scared, his head full of the doubts and demons put there by the sisters. And he played scared, scared that Ivy would make a shot and so Jesse was determined not to let that happen. The first time down the floor Ivy faced up twenty feet out on the wing, preparing to drive the first nail into our coffin. He raised the ball to his chin and found Jesse crouched in front of him, feet spread, palms facing upward, muscles taut and panting like a rabid dog. Jesse got in so close, Ivy couldn't bring his arms down. Ivy looked like a swimming pool toddler wearing Jesse around his waist like one of those inflatable swimming rings with the toy

197

head up front, in this case Sugar Bear's head. His first shot missed badly, suddenly emboldening Jesse who followed Ivy back down the floor with a look of confidence and relief. "That's right, Baby, I'm still here, all night. I ain't going nowhere."

For all their athleticism and for all the competition Northwest had faced in the Public High League they had not scouted us. All season long, while we had eyed them and studied them, the Blue Devils had focused on Vashon. That was their obstacle, their rival. They were only vaguely aware that Kirkwood was winning games in the county, oblivious to our twenty-nine game win streak. So when we hit them with full court pressure it was a total shock, facing a group of athletes just as talented as they, but synchronized and mobilized to pressure their guards and establish a pace for which they were simply not prepared. The Blue Devil guards were tall and smooth, each several inches taller than Bill and Tommy, and both skilled ball handlers. But Bayless and Jeff Zehner were distant memories. Our press was now unbeatable by dribble penetration. And Northwest Coach Jodie Bailey had failed to install a zone press break. We forced three straight turnovers, raced to a 10-2 lead and Bailey blinked first, calling a timeout to rally his flagging troops as the Kirkwood bench leapt onto the floor, coaches and players jumping and screaming. Bailey's players trudged over to him, both guards shocked and shaken, Hercle Ivy rubbing the red rash that the Jesse inner tube had already burned around his waist. From that moment, just two minutes into the game, until the very end, Jodie Bailey was playing catch up.

I don't remember much about that game. I remember plays and moments. Shortly after that first timeout I stood along the lane preparing to block out on a Northwest free throw attempt. It was just a few minutes in, anticipation still electrifying us all. The official tossed the ball to the shooter and I noticed the official was Mr. Schnell. He stepped back under the basket, as photographers lining the floor scurried aside, like minnows in a pond when you thrust your hand in. I glanced up into the three tiers of seating, fans stretching to the rafters, smoky and distant, 8,500 of them occupying every seat. They hovered over us like a horde of fishermen on the shore dropping their lines into our small pond.

"Hey Mr. Schnell," I cried over the commotion. "Have you ever been in the middle of anything like this?"

"No, Drew, never," he answered with a wry smile. I grabbed the made free throw and stepped toward him to inbound and he was already running down court. I figured he was just as conscious of the imposing hordes of black fans as I was. After more than eighty varsity games and dozens of unfavorable calls I would never quit searching for a bond or connection with him.

Late in the first quarter Bill drove into the lane, an invading cancer set to shoot or pass, to poison the opposition from within their defense. He shook his defender and sailed toward the hoop for a sure layup but Blue Devil center Ruben Shelton leapt and cupped Bill's shot in one big hand and slammed it back, bouncing the ball off Bill's head and out of bounds. Maybe he was sending a message that the lane was his,

199

no visitors allowed. But Bill just set up to play *D*, a subtle smile across his face. One door had closed but another one was sure to open; he'd figure out another way. He was on his way to eighteen points including six of seven free throws. No worries.

Early in the second quarter Jesse's smothering defense had limited Ivy to just two shots, both missed, but in his zeal to defend, Jesse went to the bench with his third foul. Free from his straight jacket, Hercle went immediately to work, making a layup and then a high arching bomb, punctuated by a high fist pump to stir the crowd. Northwest was back within three.

Rock went silently about his business, no smack talk and no spats with referees. I didn't know it at the time but he had played against most of Northwest's players during his summer sorties downtown for pickup games. Late in the second quarter Rock dribbled inside the free throw line and turned for a fade away jumper, his money shot. Up went Rock and up went Ivy, arm extended, palm open, looking to pack that shot and perhaps duplicate Shelton's head bounce maneuver. Rock hovered and Ivy kept climbing, like an eagle over its prey. Rock frowned and held it, now descending and risking a traveling violation but dead set against Ivy gaining any satisfaction or edge with a blocked shot. At the last possible second Rock launched his shot, a heave really, with no chance to make it but at least out of Ivy's reach. The ball grazed the rim and fell into Shelton's waiting hands but Rock won his mini battle as he so often did. No block for Ivy, no trash talk. In fact they ran back and it was Rock in Ivy's ear, "What are you *thinking*? You can't block my shot!". Halftime arrived and we led by eight.

Back in the St. Louis U. locker room, the marijuana smoke had dissipated and the air was clear but for sweat and intensity. Mr. Miller spoke animatedly for us to keep the pressure on their guards and be sure to rebound as a team. Each of us sat forward on our chairs listening and processing. A standing room-only crowd stomped and shouted yet none of us heard a thing but the soft rhythm of our collective breathing. We had leapt off the cliff and plunged into icy water and thrust our heads up to behold each other, frantic and alive. We had narrowed our focus to the point there was no crowd, no arena, just the Northwest Blue Devils, our targets for four months, so dominating, so intimidating and now so close at hand. We were the better team for a half, could we sustain it? We stood and crowded around Mr. Miller, hands in the middle. "Defense!" we cried, followed by nods and clinched fists as we headed out the door and back into that ominous crowd, back onto the floor to face players good enough to be our equals for the first time all season wondering if we had enough. Rock's steely stare and Jesse's determined stride suggested even if we didn't, we thought we did. Bill trailed the group, eyes glazed over, deep in thought, replaying the first half and planning the second while Tommy walked ahead, in a fog, scoreless in the first half, a nonfactor.

To start the second half Shelton was in my head. I rebounded, got position for good looks but could never get free. I had faced enough leapers to assimilate an arsenal of head fakes and footwork to get my shot but Ruben was different. He would spread out in front of me, arms down and hands ready, daring me to shoot and refusing to leave his feet for fakes. I'd seen that too. If an opponent wasn't wound tight enough to go for a fake he must be on his heels. I possessed a short jump and quick release repertoire designed to get the shot off before a patient leaper could react. But Shelton was too quick for that, altering those attempts as well. I was en route to a very poor shooting night but it wasn't nerves; it was Ruben.

Northwest fought back. They didn't break our press but they did navigate it, bringing Ivy and Shelton into the backcourt and passing it ahead through them. Midway through the third quarter they caught us and went ahead, 42-41. But the pace of the game was so fast there was no time to concern ourselves. Moulder got one right back for us. Our press was no longer the lever it had been in the first half; credit Jodie Bailey with some halftime adjustments. But Rock and I had established ourselves on the backboards on our way to eleven and fifteen rebounds respectively, while Ivy and Shelton would top Northwest with ten each. Rock punctuated each rebound with a brief observation, "That's mine," or "Get back!" his running commentary of no particular note to the Northwest players but a familiar comfort to us, sounding just like he did in Saturday pickup games at the Center. High above the floor in the top deck Sam Williams savored every rebound and every point his brother scored, tickled at their role reversals while dismissing all the questions peppered by his fellow fans, "Who is that? Is that your brother?" We led by one point after three quarters.

We broke our huddle and walked back out to start the fourth only vaguely aware of the tumult. Northwest fans behind the Kirkwood bench had harassed and threatened us all night in vain. Northwest players lined up for the center jump stoic and calm as we did the same. They had absorbed our opening haymaker and slowly, resolutely they had climbed back up. This game was too close to call and these teams were equals. I thought about what a shame it was that one would lose and miss a trip to the Final Four when either of us could wipe out any other tournament team. It was like glancing along the wall of the Center to see a bunch of marginal players owning next game. You realized this was the game and these were the opponents that made it so rewarding.

Early in the fourth quarter Ivy tried to block Rock's shot and fouled him. "You can't get that!" muttered Rock as he stepped to the line. I glanced to the scorer's table. It was Ivy's fourth foul. One more and he'd foul out. We inched back ahead and switched to a 1-2-2 zone to force them to make outside shots. With five minutes to go and Kirkwood clinging to that one point lead, Ivy head faked and Rock wanted a piece of that jumper so badly he bit, soaring into the rafters. Ivy put down his dribble, got to the baseline and rocketed for a layup and the lead. The crowd saw a blur but I saw it all in slow motion. As soon as Rock leapt I plotted Ivy's path as in a time-lapse photo. I stepped across the lane to meet him and I added it up in my head. Ivy had four fouls and I had three. Even if I drew the foul I'd still be playing. But if Ivy fouled…

Block his shot or set up to draw the charge? It was still slow motion so I pondered that one for a moment. Hell, he had hops and the experience of opposing that inner city crowd. No way I'd get his shot. He might make it and draw a foul and he was an eighty percent free throw shooter. That would be three points and all the momentum. So with a silent apology to Loose Booty I decided to play it conservatively. This was Kiel Auditorium and not the Center. It wouldn't be my call to make or defend. So I spread them out and absorbed the contact, Ivy so high in his leap I was staring at his uniform waistband as he hit me.

The crowd roared as we hit the floor and I heard the whistle, glanced up hopefully and my heart sank. Mr. Schnell! I hadn't forgotten about him but I had lost track. There had been a fifty-fifty chance for the other ref but no such luck. Damn! I stared up as he lithely danced past, his striped shirt framed by three tiers of screaming fans, whistle dancing in his mouth, taking one last glance at the heap on the floor and then hopping toward the scorer's table on one foot, the other foot kicking the air in front of him. Mr. Miller saw him coming and dropped his head, turning away at the inevitability of this call from this ref, whom he knew even better than I. It had been three years of frustration for me but probably decades for Mr. Miller.

I sat up as Ivy stood and stepped toward the foul line, Mr. Schnell now standing before the scorer's table like a contestant before a review board. One more glance back at us, at me, and he slapped his palm against the back of his head; offensive foul, charging foul; ball to Kirkwood and purgatory for Ivy. I rose and trotted up the court and looked at Mr. Schnell who stood on the sideline pounding the ball and imploring Bill to put it in play. He wouldn't return my gaze and in fact we never exchanged another word or look for the remainder of the game after which I would never see him again.

Why? After all of the no-calls and all of my fruitless pleas, why this once? Why now? Why here? He did not give in to the game or the crowd. He had made more than his share of calls against Kirkwood this night. Maybe I had finally performed a charge to his satisfaction, although I could count dozens where I had set up sooner and drawn better contact. Or perhaps I had met my Schnell quota, twenty or thirty or however many so that he had thought ahead and said if Drew steps out there one more time he gets the call. I've had a lot of time to think about that one and I've decided it came down to the game. It wasn't about Mr. Schnell or Drew or KHS and Northwest, simply the game; you and me and a ball. Ivy was Northwest's horse and I was ours. We were locked up in a tense duel and Ivy tested me. I'm going to the rack and what are you going to do about it?

Ivy glared at Schnell and trudged to the bench, angry at the call and I thought, "Damn it had to be slow motion for you just as it was for me. You had time to count up your fouls and to size up the terrain. You knew I was coming. If you thought I was going to let you go, that's your fault. And by thinking you could jump past me that was your fate, and your team's."

That was a senior moment for me. As a sophomore I'd never have reacted quickly enough to contest the shot and as a junior I'd have tried to block it, likely to no avail. But as a senior I possessed the experience of so many moments like that one, so many templates of success. In the forty years since that moment I have told the story of that one play dozens of times as a lesson in what I now preach as the three P's: Patience, Persistence and Perseverance. I have taught children the importance of cultivating others; particularly authority figures and I have utilized cantankerous officials as my example. "You have to abide by their rules," I say. "You have to learn to deal with them and win them over." After decades in professional sales I look back on Mr. Schnell as my first customer. He finally bought what I was selling.

Ivy was finished. But one glorious facet of the game is the opportunity for greatness it so randomly provides. Ruben Shelton had toiled in Ivy's shadow all season. A junior, he was deprived of his sophomore year of eligibility for having enrolled at Northwest High which was outside of Ruben's school district. He had wanted to play for Jodie Bailey, for a winning program so he took the advice of others and ignored the rules and paid for it with a year of banishment. So he was on no one's radar screen when his junior season began. But he was a great player, smart and athletic, destined for All Metro recognition his senior year and a full ride to Kansas University. And the moment Ivy sat down Ruben stood up, striding across the Kiel Auditorium floor and taking it as his own. The Blue Devils would run things through him the rest of the way and he responded with jump shots, rebounds, layups and his continuing defense against me. Shelton's layup with 1:13 to go put Northwest ahead, 65-63.

Most teams call timeout at times like that but we were taught to grab it and go. A pass to Moulder, a drive to the hoop and a miss but it happened so fast I beat Shelton to the rebound and put it back in before he could get there. With the game tied,

206

Northwest chose to run the clock down for the last shot. We remained in our zone and when Shelton faced up in front of the KHS bench, it was our reserve forward, Steve Schaper guarding him along the baseline. He head faked, but Schaper didn't go for it so Shelton put down a dribble, dropped a shoulder and started around. It was slow motion again and I could already see my move to draw the charge. Mr. Schnell had to give me this one because it was identical to the Ivy one and he couldn't change his criteria now. We'd get possession and then a win.

Schaper slid over but he was late. "Let him go!" I hollered. But Steve already shoved a knee out, trying to stop Shelton but tripping him instead. It was an easy call, foul on Schaper, Shelton to the line shooting one-and-one. Northwest called timeout and I walked past Ruben, staring straight into his eyes, searching for nerves or doubt. His eyes met mine and didn't quaver. A mere trace of a smile parted his lips. "See you back at the free throw line," he seemed to say. "Ballgame".

The giant arena clock above the court showed eight seconds to go and I craned my neck to look into the Northwest huddle while Mr. Miller hollered. "Miss or make, no timeout. Get it ahead and get a shot." There was no play call, no scheme. Just do what we did every day in every practice. Get it out and run. This was why he had drilled us over and over. "Rogers!" he growled one last time. "No timeout! Just go!"

I lined up taking the inside position on the right. I always took that spot because on a make I could grab it moving to my right, step out and inbound with my right hand, my strong hand. Rock lined up opposite me ready to block out and

207

contest the rebound but knowing to let me have it on a make so I could get it to my right hand. Shelton took the ball from the ref, holding it and staring at it like a freshly opened box on Christmas day, eyes wide and marveling. "He's nervous," I thought.

Shelton spun the ball in both hands, whirling it like a Vegas slot machine, then catching it and spreading his feet. He glanced at the basket and then at me, then back at the basket. "He's not nervous," I admitted to myself. "This one's in." There was the bend, extend and swish. Really good shooters splash the net and this was a deluge. I glanced at Mr. Miller. How about a timeout now, to break his rhythm? My coach stood, arms crossed and foot tapping like a tardy commuter waiting for the bus. No retreat, no respite. Get it and go, dammit!

That first one was the hard one, the front end of a one-and-one. Miss it and Kirkwood gets overtime at worst and a last shot victory at best. Make it and you're in control. Plus you've conquered your nerves and the moment. Second one's easy. Ruben took it from the ref, same routine, and I stared past him at our two guards. Moulder stood hands on hips, feigning indifference but inching toward me, ready to take an inbounds pass and dribble up. He'd get something, quality shot or not, he'd get something. Robert began talking a stream of trash to Shelton who gazed placidly ahead, undaunted. Out at midcourt, Scott Markle was flanked by both Northwest guards. Markle inched closer too, shadowed by those guards. Beyond the three of them lay a half court of open hardwood and our basket.

Shelton cocked it in his hands as Moulder stared down at his own sneakers, frustrated at the inevitability of our plight. "Tomorrow these will be baseball cleats," Bill thought to himself. The clock wouldn't start until it hit the rim on a miss or we inbounded after a make. I stared at Shelton and watched his release. It was off, not by much, but he pulled it left just a little. I'd seen misses like that a thousand times. It was going to hit the rim inside left, then the backboard and bounce off right, to my side. I knew it.

I blocked out my man as the ball hit. I knew to leap quickly or it'd clear my hands and bounce to Northwest. I grabbed it right off the backboard, grabbing it with both hands like I'd been taught. Seven seconds. Moulder stepped forward clapping his hands, demanding the ball as Rock pushed back against both Northwest rebounders, clearing space, vital space for me to raise it and pass. I stepped to my right and shot a quick glance to midcourt. Markle had stepped forward and was pointing down at the center circle and both Northwest guards were staring down like he'd pointed out buried treasure. Incredible.

And then Scott was gone, spinning and sprinting away, head back over his shoulder with a look of utter glee, like he'd gotten the last cookie and no one was going to take it from him. Both Blue Devil guards looked up and turned to chase. Markle had created space but not much. I lined him up, calculating the chances of hitting him as Moulder hollered for the ball. Take a chance on Scott or hope that Bill could dribble up and get a shot? No time to think as I raised my arm. Six seconds.

209

I let it go long, using a looming Shelton as my peep sight. Markle had two steps on them and that's all we ever got in practice, all of those practices, countless repetitions, get it out, throw ahead, push, push, push. This was just another drill, except for one thing, the urgency of the moment. I rushed the pass just a little, turning my right hand inside, putting unwanted spin on it and sending it curving left to right. I started it out right toward Markle's head but as it sailed over Northwest's guards it tailed badly, forcing Scott to veer out to catch it over his right shoulder and then try to dribble back left to get to the hoop.

That it was "Sparkle" Markle out there instead of Tommy was fate. Tommy had gone zero for seven shooting and labored through a dismal game, undoubtedly preoccupied with his father. Mr. Miller had removed him halfway through the fourth quarter. Though he was a backup, Markle was probably our fastest, most athletic guard, perhaps the only one who could make that tough of a catch with the balance to recover and dribble toward the basket. He was certainly the only one brave enough for what came next.

Five seconds. Markle stretched out to his right, caught it and threw down a dribble, planting his outside foot and lunging back left, back toward the basket. The Northwest guards closed in, fueled by desperation, anything to protect that one point lead. A second dribble and Scott glanced back, seeing the Blue Devils bearing down, their arms outstretched, reeling him in. Up he went, a fox leaping for home ahead of the rabid hounds.

They got him. As Scott extended toward the rim they both got their hands on him, grabbing his waist and legs,

210

frantically pawing at anything they could get to stop that shot. The ball in his palm, the rim a few feet away, Scott hovered in midair and felt his feet pulling from beneath him. He was now parallel with the court, six feet up and certain to crash.

There was still time to save himself. We've all been there, hands full of some chore, balance lost, choosing between salvaging the task while hurting ourselves or bailing out and lowering our arms to break the fall in self preservation. I'd have bailed; I think most anyone would have. It's instinct, a fear of falling wired into our DNA.

Up came his feet and out stretched his arm as he sailed headlong under the backboard and toward the iron stanchion beyond. Then came a flick of the wrist, a final abdication of self, a defining commitment to the moment and to the game. Four seconds.

I saw it drop through. I didn't see the collision. The officials raced to the heap of players and chose one of the Northwest guards to whistle for the foul. There had been nothing dirty, no intention to injure, just anxiety and desperation to stop that shot. Markle lay against the stanchion, knocked cold from his head hitting the iron base. Timeout Northwest. Our team trainer, Clay Slover helped Scott to the bench, pressing a towel to the gash on his forehead. They laid him down behind the bench as bedlam erupted and projectiles sailed over us: drinks, cushions and chairs. We huddled together, covering our heads and exchanging wild looks, stunned. "That's their last timeout!" barked Mr. Miller. "Contest them up court but don't foul!"

211

Tommy replaced Markle and stepped to the line for the free throw, Kirkwood now up one. Northwest had ninety feet to negotiate and no timeouts. The rest of us gathered at midcourt. There was no need to rebound the free throw, just prevent anything easy on our end. Tommy stood at the far free throw line, his back to us, alone, staring up at the glass backboard and into the raucous crowd beyond. I wondered what he saw right then. Was he even in this building; was he even in this game? For all of his athleticism and intensity, for all of his toughness, at that moment Tommy Grice looked like an abandoned orphan on a city corner with nowhere left to go. Everyone had contributed that night but him, until then. He drained it. At a time before three point shots he had ensured us overtime at worst, even if Northwest somehow made a hoop. He slapped his thigh and backed up toward us, ready to defend.

The crowd roared and edged toward the court. I was reminded of summer days as a kid when we'd play in the neighborhood and suddenly we noticed dark clouds gathering in the distance and then a rush of wind setting the maple trees dancing. Another gust of wind and you could smell the rain and hear the gentle patter on the leaves. You knew you had about a minute before the downpour. A wet wind blew across the court and the dark clouds were descending upon us, filled for a deluge. Northwest inbounded to Shelton at midcourt and no one challenged him. Three seconds. He put down a dribble, gaining momentum toward the basket and closing to within about thirty-five feet. Two seconds. I ran at him. He picked up his dribble and lined it up, legs bent, ready to launch. I ran past him,

212

a safe three feet of margin and yelled, "Hey!" One second. He let it go and I stopped dead, looking right over his shoulder. It was right on line.

The shot hit the back of the rim and bounded away at the buzzer. And that was it, game over. No celebration, no thoughts of the Final Four, just retreat. Kiel Auditorium exploded into utter mayhem. Bottles and chairs hit the floor as maddened thugs rushed us from all sides. The police were overwhelmed as punches flew and victims hit the ground. I'd have liked to shake their hands, to have told Shelton and Ivy just how much I respected them and what a thrill it had been to play this game and share these moments. I saw them both sprinting away toward their locker room, arms over their heads and ducking debris, experienced riot victims who knew when to turn and run.

Mr. Miller shouted at us, herding us toward the aisle leading back to our locker room as the mob spilled across the court. The torrent intensified as we shoved our way through the fists, elbows and flying debris and I glanced upward to the rafters. The entire arena pulsated as fights broke out everywhere. My parents were up there along with my brother and my grandparents too. Heaven help them, I thought. We escaped the outer seating and made our way up a large tunnel among smaller clusters of fans. Rock walked ahead of us, singing and shouting, ecstatic and defiant. Several Northwest toughs ran ahead, grabbing him by the arm and spinning him around. "Why are you coming down here and playing against us?" shouted one.

"Take your goddamn hands off me!" hollered Rock, wrenching free and clenching his fists. "I ain't playing for none of you! I'm just playing to win!" We pushed inside to the safety of our locker room, giddy from the victory and the perilous journey to safety. I spoke with a newspaper reporter who then turned to grab a word with Mr. Miller and quickly the room settled. I glanced around at my teammates, my family. Rock stood clowning with his buddy, Locker Room Smith. Twenty points and eleven rebounds for Rock. Jesse sat hunched over, elbows on his knees staring into his locker, exhausted from the effort put forth in holding Ivy ten points below his season average. Tommy was out of his uniform and into the shower without a word, alone with his thoughts. Bill tugged off his sneakers, basking in the realization that he'd have them on again tomorrow and not his baseball cleats. Eighteen points and a dozen assists for the Thrill. Scott Markle was helped toward the door for a trip to the Emergency Room and stitches. Jesse congratulated him and reminded him we were headed to the Final Four but Scott couldn't piece it together. Mr. Miller chatted with the reporter and stepped outside for a cigarette. There had been no last second play to conjure, no in-game adjustments. He had drilled us for two years, get it out and go, until it was instinct, until it came down to that night.

The next morning the school hallways were electrified with students babbling about the victory and their individual stories of the riot and their various escapes. Some had fought their way out of Kiel and others offered eyewitness accounts of muggings inside and out of that arena. Blacks and whites, students and adults, nearly every Kirkwood fan had been threatened or attacked. The morning paper had quoted Jodie Bailey who said, "...a heck of a way to go out, to lose on a fluke like that." Bill and I sat at a table during free period no longer wondering about and plotting against Northwest, Bailey's words fresh in our minds. We had led that game for thirty of the thirty-two minutes played, we had scored the first basket and the last; we were the better team. Bill smiled and went into his Denver Miller routine. "Hell you could play us all night and we'd still win," he growled.

The bell rang ending the class period and I headed off to lunch, passing by Hollywood and Vine. Half a dozen sisters stood waiting, easing up to me to flirt. "Hey Drew!" "How you doin'?" "Good game last night, you look cute in those shorts." Here was your fluke, Jodie Bailey, these black girls treating me so sweetly. It would last for maybe another day before the pack regrouped and the smiles reverted to snarls. I quickened my pace, turned a corner and vowed to find an alternate route to the cafeteria, to avoid Hollywood and Vine, I knew survival was pretty high on Maslow's list.

The Sugar Bear swim toy #30, obscuring Hercle Ivy

I'm head faking but Ruben Shelton refuses to bite.

Chapter 11

Jesse's toss catches Stolle flat-footed so as I rise it's just me - no other players can get to it. This is it, the all-state center with the game in my hands. He put it right where I want it, slightly toward the rim and over my head but as I jump there's nothing there, no spring, no magic. I'm just another player raking my arm at a ball I'm not going to reach. I land as Raytown players surround the loose ball and I wonder how in the world I missed that pass. Jesse put it where he always does but I was six inches short in my jump. They grab it and dribble into the frontcourt and proceed to stall, a two-point lead and time on their side. We chase the ball but we're exhausted, mentally and physically. It's been such an ordeal, trying to establish our pace, trying to cut those puppet strings, trying to extricate ourselves. We've been scaling a mountain whose summit is enclosed in clouds, no sign of the end, no salvation, only our failing grip on a polished slope.

They toss it around, stalling away the final seconds and I think back on the tempo of this game as well as control. Geppetto's used every timeout available to him, each one strategically called to stop or prevent a run. The refs have been no help. They're anonymous, from some unknown

218

conference so I don't know them and neither does Mr. Miller. There's no one to appeal to. The Raytown crowd was in charge here long before we took the court, almost like older kids who took the playground before us, keeping score and refusing to call it a game until their team led. The Raytown players have toyed with us, never engaging, only jabbing and dodging. This entire game has been a dull ache, initially masked by our energy and determination; an ache that began early and slowly began to intensify. For two hours now we've explored it, searching for its roots, for the cause and for the antidote. It is so pervasive that we can't eradicate it no matter how hard we try. We have tried to run and tried to press but the ache is woven into the fabric of this game. So we fought it, employing the athleticism we were blessed with and the training and tactics we were given, railing against it like unruly children, twisting and writhing but it has us by the sleeve and all we are doing is spending ourselves to no avail. I cast a quick glance at Mr. Miller standing in front of our bench, arms crossed, our subs sitting forward, hands locked, staring forlornly through hollow eyes. All season long we've been show animals, prancing proudly before admiring audiences. But now we are reduced to so many stupid dogs chasing a game of catch among our masters, tongues hanging and eyes wide but vacant, running ourselves ragged. We have run all season and we won't stop now, not even as the clock ticks down, mercilessly shoving us to our fate. I look around at my fellow victims, my teammates, and watch their shoulders sag and their wills depart because finally and

219

*fatally we are forced to accept the one eventuality we swore
we would never abide. There is nothing we can do.*

The End

> And as the gloom begins to fall
> I see there is no, only all
> Though you came with sword held high
> You did not conquer, only die
> —"Conquistador", Procol Harum

I lay sprawled across a pair of seats at the very
back of our chartered bus, my head propped against the
worn leather gym bag staring blankly into the night.
Distant hilltops slipped slowly by, interrupted by an
occasional town or gas station, car lights sporadically
flashing through the window, racing along the ceiling
and then off into the night, like thieves. A silent shroud
encased the inside of the bus, broken only by the muted
hum of the big tires against the pavement of Interstate
70. Players sought refuge up and down the aisle,
hunched over alone in the darkness like chastened
children banished to their rooms. I was glad to be
headed home that night and not languishing in our
hotel.

We had boarded this bus just a day earlier,
exiting our Friday classes in the late morning and
gathering in the school parking lot as a voice through a

megaphone introduced each one of us to a gathering of students and we climbed the stairs into the bus, one or two players pausing at the top stair to turn and wave like dignitaries. I think we had begun to unravel right then, as our settled routine gave way to the Game. I had never pictured it like that, a bus gathering us up and transporting us out of town, to a hotel and to games in Brewer Field House. I had pictured Kiel Auditorium, downtown St. Louis and the ghosts of past Final Fours. When had they decided to move it all to Columbia, MO?

We had arrived in Columbia mid-day, napped in our rooms and then taken the floor that night for our semifinal against a team so foreign to us we still didn't know their school name even after we won. We were distracted by the hotel, the restaurant and the gym as well as by each other, Rock roaming the hotel hallways singing "Break Up to Make Up" and Tommy making phony phone calls to our rooms and hanging up. I knew those guys on the court but not off of it and the trip seemed to magnify our differences, not bridge them.

Saturday morning we had awoken, far from home and our routine. Saturday mornings usually meant familiar, energetic runs at the Center, absorption with the game and freedom from the Game. Instead we sat in a corner of the hotel restaurant, local papers strewn around proclaiming the Game and the matchup, undefeated Kirkwood against tournament-tested Raytown South as we wondered who Raytown even was. I thought longingly of the Center and Ricky Nelson's haunting chant, "Pull Chollie!"

We had ridden away confident in ourselves and sure of our destiny. But we were as wrong as the second place plaque tossed rudely onto a seat up front near Mr. Miller. I hadn't looked at it, hadn't touched it. The formal presentation ceremony immediately following the game was short and sweet, just as it should have been. The night and the first place trophy belonged to Raytown South. Had it been that first place trophy riding home with us I still wouldn't have coveted it. It was the game we had played for, not the trophy. Someone once said that championships should be rewarded with bananas to be eaten on the spot, savored and then discarded like the banana peel. I liked that expression, even before we settled for second banana.

The Raytown crowd was still celebrating on the floor as we slunk away like villains toward our locker room. Once inside there was nothing to say. No one looked around, embarrassed as we were to have failed each other and ourselves. We were absolute strangers.

Raytown was a good team with good players. None of them ever said a word during the game, busily going about their business, dismantling us. Geppetto was an outstanding coach; hell this had been his second state championship in three years, great program. Folks were already saying if we played Raytown ten times we'd beat them nine; this had just been their night. I didn't care enough to ponder that. I was pretty sure Raytown would disagree anyway. They had a plan that they executed. Why wouldn't they figure they could execute it, and us, again? Besides, the game was over.

Pickup games last until there's no one left. Players come and go and individual games are won and lost but the game continues as long as there are players. Winners hold the court and losers go home. Oftentimes, after hours and hours, two teams are playing it out. The game is close and suddenly you realize there's nobody left waiting, no one's got next. When your game ends everyone will go home. So someone says hey let's keep going to fifteen straight and because no one's waiting it's agreed. It doesn't matter whether you're winning or losing at that point; you just want to play on. It's like reading a book that's so good you don't want it to end so you slow it down, maybe even put it aside and glance at it each night but refuse to open it back up because when you do you know it's done.

So the tears I shed in the back of that darkened bus were not for losing the state championship or that one game. I cried because it was over. As we drew nearer to home I sat up and strained to see Mr. Miller, way up front, sitting just behind the driver, surrounded by empty rows of seats, alone. Despite the newspaper stories and his own occasional musings I had never given much credence to his story, to his failure to ever win a state championship. But I thought about it that night.

I realized that for all of my fixation and fascination with the game, I was still a kid. Someday you grow up and then you grow old and when the string of games grows long enough it represents a lifetime and within that lifetime most of us have goals and for Mr. Miller one of those was to win The Game just once. But he didn't then and perhaps he never would and I wondered just what he had accomplished and what I might have learned from him. He was not a father or a mentor to me. But he was an example, an example of grace and determination.

Grace was the way he handled that late night crowd on the back of a flatbed truck in the KHS parking lot in the wee hours of the morning after our wretched defeat. We shuffled off the bus and dabbed at our tears and disappointment and nearly four hundred faithful fans stared up at him and awaited his words. Our team stood speechless, that one decisive defeat muting our youthful vigor and boundless futures while Mr. Miller, wearing an albatross of immense proportions around his thick neck, with his resources nearly spent and his prospects so diminished, stepped forward. His voice cracked and he covered it with a muffled cough. Then he cleared his throat, took a deep breath and spoke to the crowd and to us about effort and virtue and opportunity, raising our spirits even while his must have been spent. He sent us home proud and fulfilled though I wondered what he had left for himself when he got home.

As for determination, I learned about that the following Monday when he gathered us all for the final time in his classroom. I sat there feeling sorry for him, angry at myself for having failed to deliver him his chalice and lamenting the fact that he would never again have as good a shot as he had with our team. I watched him rise from his desk, thank the seniors for our contributions and wish us well as we left him behind with the underclassmen. Before the door had shut behind us I heard him say to his remaining group, "Boys, I think we can be as good next year as we were this year and I think we can win the state championship." I thought to myself how delusional he was, how he couldn't possibly duplicate this year's success. I walked to my car and drove home thinking how strong Mr. Miller was to give that kind of direction and hope to Rock, Bill and the rest. But without Tommy, Jesse, Rhein and me there was no way they'd be that good the next year. But they were. And damn if they didn't make it back to the state championship game where they took the floor as favorites once again.

But that's a whole other story.

Epilogue

I've thought back to that state championship game a few times, mostly pleasant musings about this play or that. One thing that puzzled me was how I never got any touches during those final few minutes. Years passed and I got hold of a grainy film of that game. I watched that film half a dozen times still baffled over my lack of opportunities down the stretch. It wasn't until writing this book that I pored over that film second by second and discovered three great looks I had in that fourth quarter, all misses and all forgotten. A scorer truly only remembers the makes.

The game is a magnet and back in those days its pull was strong enough to hold our group together through all of what society and competition put in our way. But it is not eternal. Times change and teams disband.

Ruben Shelton earned All State recognition the following season, leading Northwest High School back to the state tournament. He attended Kansas University on a basketball scholarship. He now practices law in St. Louis and has been active in a number of community organizations. He and his wife have been married for

226

thirty-three years. I spoke with Ruben during the writing of this book and hung up from that one conversation having renewed a friendship I never would have known but for the game.

Hercle Ivy played four stellar years of Big Eight basketball at Iowa State and led the Big Eight in scoring in 1975. He now lives and works in the St. Louis area.

Jodie Bailey coached high school basketball for 42 seasons and accumulated a record of 828 wins and 198 losses and was inducted into the Missouri Sports Hall of Fame in 1989.

Bud Lathrop, aka "Geppetto" was the first boys' basketball coach at Raytown South, from its opening in 1964 until he retired in 2006. His teams compiled a record of 955-301 and won state titles in 1970, 1972, 1977 and 1990. He lives in the Kansas City area and is still in touch with most of the players from his 1972 team including Ed Stolle, who earned a basketball scholarship to the University of Missouri. Bud was kind enough to provide a good deal of background and perspective for me while researching this book. We concluded our phone conversation, each still convinced that his was the better team.

During my college years I'd occasionally wander up to the Center. I played ball with the whole crew of characters that sometimes included Tommy, Jesse and Robert. I moved from the St. Louis area immediately after graduating college and away from that part of my life forever. After KHS, Jesse Jackson remained in the St. Louis area where he still resides. I saw him once after I moved, at a KHS reunion of our team. He was the same old Sugar Bear.

Robert Williams played one year of junior college basketball at Meramec Community College in St. Louis, and now lives and works in North St. Louis. I saw Rock at a KHS alumni basketball game and at the KHS reunion for our team. Rock was a willing contributor to this book as we spoke by phone several times. He talks more fondly about the pickup games he found driving around St. Louis with his crew than about those high school games. He says he can still whup anybody.

I have not seen Tommy Grice since high school. I spoke with him briefly by phone one time regarding the book. He lives and works in the St. Louis area.

Bill Moulder and I have remained close friends all our lives. He played four years of basketball at St. Louis University setting a record for career assists. He has fashioned a hugely successful career working for a motivation and travel incentive company in the St. Louis area, one that has taken him to all fifty states and dozens of countries around the world. Despite opportunities to live anywhere, he chose to remain in Kirkwood where he and his wife raised three sons, all of whom attended KHS. He has been a driving force behind my effort to write and publish this book.

228

Denver Miller spent his entire coaching career at Kirkwood High School amassing 790 victories in more than one thousand total games coached. He retired in 1977 after taking five teams to the state Final Four, including state final appearances in 1950, 1962, 1972 and 1973. He lived out his remaining years in Kirkwood where he was a fixture at Greenbrier Country Club, holding court in a back room playing cards and telling stories. Mr. Miller passed away in 1988 at the age of 76. He never won a state championship.

I attended Kansas University on a four-year basketball scholarship but transferred after my freshman year. My sophomore year I played at Meramec Community College and that was the end of college ball for me. I graduated from the University of Missouri and began a career in sales management, moving to the east coast, then to Houston and finally to Southern California where I currently reside. Through all of those relocations and all of the overnight travel I never lacked for companions. I would play ball at a local gym or playground court, never failing to strike up a bond thanks to the game.

Earl Monroe said, "If you don't play ball you can't hang out." I kept playing and hanging out until my fifth knee surgery when the cumulative arthritis finally forced me to quit, but not before I had logged hundreds and hundreds of games and associated

229

friendships. I clung to the game through coaching youth basketball, always amused that parents would thank me for coaching their kids when it was I who benefitted more than they. My wife said that giving up hoop changed me and I think, "How could it not"?

Maybe the writing of this book was an exorcism. At the very least it provides an answer to the riddle of my life: What is stronger than racism, as enduring as life, addictive enough to grind one's knees to sawdust, and pervasive enough to haunt a middle aged man's dreams?

The game.

Made in the USA
Charleston, SC
08 June 2013